This book is presented with

Robert Moten, Sr., and Eliza Moten. Thank you for planting the

seed and providing me with the courage and inspiration to bloom.

TABLE OF CONTENTS

FOREWORD

Imagine being asked to participate in a game with the potential to win unlimited fortunes. The prize for the winner is a lifetime of happiness, health, wealth and success. Imagine being asked to sit at a table and play this game without being told the rules. The prize is substantial and you want a chance at winning so you are going to play despite not knowing the rules. You find yourself stumbling through the game, missing out on opportunities and returning to the starting point all because you are clueless to the strategies. In an effort to gain some advantage to winning, you begin to observe others playing. You observe their particular strategies and nuances and begin incorporating them in your play, totally unaware that they, like you, have not been privy to the rules. They are just as clueless as you. Here you stand, at a table full of people playing a game with the highest stakes imaginable and no one's winning because no one has a playbook.

Life is a game we were all thrust into. If you are like me, you have stumbled through it, learning as you go along hoping that what you have learned will give you some advantage. There may be times you feel you've mastered the game, then there are the times when the game is no longer enjoyable because you keep landing on the same undesirable squares, losing your turn and watching others continually pass you by. You become frustrated because you feel the hand you've been dealt or the dice you've rolled makes it virtually impossible to win. The big payout, happiness, health, wealth and success, that we all desire appears to be out of your reach. What you weren't told is, contrary to other games you've participated in, everyone can indeed be a winner in the game of life.

Consider this book your playbook with the rules and strategies that will transform the hand you are currently playing with into a winning one and load the dice with a propensity toward success. The first requirement is to be willing to disregard many of the rules and strategies that you've naively incorporated along the way. Be willing to set aside the reality that has had your attention for quite some time and be willing to give attention to that which will lead to the big payout.

There is one common thread that runs through all of us. Regardless of our background or our cultural or religious affiliation, we all desire to be happy. Most of us have experienced, at one time or another, a sense of happiness. For some, the experience may have been fleeting; others have experienced it for longer durations. Regardless of your personal experience, we all tend to agree that once a person has experienced that wondrous feeling of happiness, that desire to experience more and more of it for longer periods of time is activated. It is at this crucial time in a person's life, when they have decided to obtain more happiness and fulfillment that one of two things may occur: They either began to experience more joy and bliss in their lives for longer periods of time or they may encounter stumbling blocks or a whole mountain of obstacles to their happiness which causes them to abort their whole attempt and adopt the belief that the pursuit of happiness is just that—a pursuit never to be reached. After years of discontent and disappointment, they have reached a point where they resign to accept things as is. They throw in the towel and adopt a gray-scale existence.

We live in a world today, where far too many people have adopted the latter belief. They exist in a life in which they have accepted a basic flat line existence. Peaks of joy are appreciated, but they are seen as just fleeting. The return to a flat line, mediocre existence is almost a relief, because the last thing they want is to activate that desire for happiness again. After a lifetime of disappointment after disappointment, they believe it is far better to accept things as they are than to hope for something more and be continually disappointed when it is not fulfilled. They convince themselves that taking the familiar road of unfulfillment is better than changing their course and embarking upon uncharted territories. They lull themselves into compromise telling themselves that happiness is just some nine letter word that has no tangible meaning. It is this belief and practice of not striving for more in fear of disappointment that has created the great divide between people who experience life as a constant struggle and those who appear to always come out on top, winning in the game of life and living lives that others believe is unattainable.

WHAT IF YOU'VE HAD IT ALL WRONG?

I once heard a story of an old man in his eighties. He had lived a good life by most people's standards. As the old man lay in his bed, death was near. In fact, if you looked hard enough, you could see the imprint of death's grip on his shoulders.

As the old man lay dying, his devoted wife of nearly 60 years sat at his deathbed. She stroked his gray hair while providing reassuring words. The man's children, grandchildren, neighbors and friends all came to visit him one last time. Their comments echoed each other. Visitor after visitor praised the man for the good life he lived. They told him, "Bob, you should be so proud of yourself. You went to the military at the tender age of 18 and served your country. You've been married to the same woman for more than half a century. You raised a family. You worked hard and retired from the same employer after 40 years. You should be so proud of yourself."

After days of a steady stream of visitors echoing this same sentiment again and again, the old man, in his last moments of life, managed to muster up enough strength to raise himself up, and in the last breath that left his body, he desperately asked, "But what if I had it all wrong?"

Is the current course of your life one that will have you questioning in your last breath, "What if I had it all wrong?" What if the principles, rules and limits you have been conditioned to believe don't hold true? What if you've done all the things that you were told were the right things to do, yet you've found yourself living an unfulfilled life?

We are living in a time when many are asking, "What if I've got it all wrong?" as evident by the personal and collective crisis that exists around us. Daily news reports are saturated with bleak updates on financial collapses. Rates of depression and anxiety disorders are higher than they've ever been. Many are in physical crisis with unhealthy bodies, unprecedented rates of obesity in both adults and children, and stress related disorders that are wreaking havoc on physical and mental well being. Millions more are in emotional crisis with failing marriages and families in turmoil.

Far too many have accepted a flat line existence. The fear of taking action to radically transform their lives takes over. There are others who may very well conjure the nerve to embark on the first steps of change only to lose that nerve right at the point radical transformation is about to occur. As you read this book, it is my sincere desire that you begin to ask yourself the "What if" questions. What if happiness can become the set point in your life? What if it is possible for you to achieve that far-fetched goal that has eluded you? What if life doesn't have to be a constant struggle? What if true happiness and fulfillment is within your reach? Even if fear has stagnated you or you've thrown in the towel just short of victory you can and will find success when you incorporate these seven steps of transformation and allow yourself to bloom.

You must decide that your desire for an extraordinary life is far more appealing than the familiarity you may feel in your current situation. The allure of that new and exciting career must outweigh the security you feel in your dead-end, non-stimulating job. The passion and bliss of a compatible, passionate relationship has to be more of a motivator than the familiarity of the mate you've been tolerating for years. The image you conjure of yourself walking tall and strong after losing the excess weight has to be more of a draw than going home and flopping in front of the TV with a bowl of ice cream. Transformation isn't easy, but with the right tools and a shift in attitude it is ALWAYS possible.

CHAPTER ONE

STEP 1: REDISCOVERING YOU

"He who knows others is learned. He who knows himself is wise."

~ Lao Tzu

THE DISCONNECT

As naive, innocent, non-resistant children, we connect with what feels good to us. There is a general quality of self-knowing in children that exists, our default setting is one of joy and bliss. Then, inevitably, the demands of life are thrust upon us and before we have the opportunity to gain a secure understanding of who we are, life begins to weaken the innate knowledge we had about ourselves. We then spend the rest of our lives trying unsuccessfully to reconnect to that part of ourselves that holds the key to our success and happiness. For many of us, before we are ever given a chance to figure out who we are, others have begun feeding us with messages of who we ought to be. As children, we were all too often placed into roles not of our choosing and not necessarily consistent with our true nature. Parents, caregivers, teachers and peers have all played a role in labeling us with descriptors not of our choosing.

Take a few moments and think about the labels affixed to you while growing up. Some of you may have been labeled the smart one, the lazy one, the fat one, the skinny one, the needy one, the strong one, the dependable one. Perhaps your label was that of the good girl, the bad boy or the one that would never amount to anything. Or, perhaps you were labeled the mistake, the troublemaker, the short-tempered one, the liar or cheat, or the one that would end up just like your mother or father. The possibilities of what you may have been labeled are infinite, and unfortunately so are the consequences.

It is no surprise that as naive, innocent children, we begin to unconsciously condition ourselves to play the roles of the labels we've been tagged with. Much like the nametags we place on our clothing when we attend some sort of conference or event, we begin to identify with our labels and approach the world as such. It is at this moment that the infinite knowing about ourselves that was present at our birth and in the innocence of early childhood is lost. We begin to play out the role of our labels and someone's limited belief about us becomes our self-fulfilling prophecy. As we embrace these labels they vehemently adhere to us and begin taking growth like a malignant tumor, infiltrating the very essence of our being. This is how the disconnect begins.

Many of you are still approaching everyday life with the residue of labels stuck boldly across your forehead. These labels aren't visible to the naked eye and they don't miraculously fall off because you enter into adulthood and are free to embrace more independence and autonomy. Even those who may appear to have it all are often covering their wounds from early labeling. They may appear to have all the trappings of fulfillment, yet they are really masking their own disconnect from their true self. These labels, once affixed, influence their every thought and behavior resulting in an inability to live authentically. Their true, authentic self is a prisoner of war held captive by early conditioning.

Then there are other wounded victims of this labeling system who don't even attempt to go so far as to fool others that they are miserable. Their hurt and disconnect is obvious to anyone who comes into contact with them. The direct and collateral damage of disconnecting with who they are has resulted in tangible ramifications ranging from such things as depression, anxiety, drug addiction, obesity, domestic abuse, etc. Countless victims of early labeling have basically checked-out, experiencing life in a hazy fog with no idea of how to escape the gray area that is their life. They are clueless to the fact that they can, at any given moment, begin to peel off the layers upon layers of labels that maintain their discontent and begin rediscovering their true self.

STEP 1: REDISCOVERING YOU

It is time to reconnect with the true essence of your being that has always been present, but has been laying dormant. It doesn't matter if it was the first seconds or first 10 years of your life that the disconnect occurred. Peeling away the labels and rediscovering the you that is capable, whole and happy is possible and imperative if you truly desire to live a fulfilling life.

MY DISCONNECT

My disconnect began just seconds after making my introduction to the world. If the first few seconds of your life is any indication of what your life will entail, then it is not surprising that it would come at a time in my life when I would have to peel away my labels. At the moment of my birth, the doctors delivering me announced to my mother that she and my father were the proud parents of a baby boy.

My mother was ecstatic. With two daughters already, she and my father had been hoping for a boy and it appeared that their prayers were answered. Hours later in the recovery room, my mother awakened to a nurse handing her the Moten family's new bundle of joy.

"Baby girl Moten," the nurse announced.

"Baby boy Moten," my mother corrected.

"No sweetie," the nurse countered, holding me up for my mother to see, "You had a girl. You lost consciousness in the delivery room and must have gotten a bit confused. You have a beautiful baby girl."

At that very moment, my father breathlessly burst into the room, holding cigars in one hand and a brand new football in the other. He beamed with pride as he prepared to get a look at his namesake.

He, too, was told by the hospital staff at the time of my birth that his wife had given birth to a boy.

As the nurse transferred me into my mother's reluctant arms, my father immediately noticed the look of confusion on his wife's face. Simultaneously, as if on the same thought frequency, my parents began unrolling me from the tight swaddle I was wrapped in tearing off my diaper. I was indeed a girl. I can only imagine how heavy my father's heart sunk down to his size 13 shoes. His coveted son was not to be, not this time around.

Despite the obvious error, this early label of baby boy Moten managed to infiltrate my early existence. I spent the first decade of my life being the quintessential tomboy and daddy's girl all rolled into one. I don't recall my father ever communicating or demonstrating any disappointment in me not being a boy, but as far back as I can remember, the mix-up at my birth was an entertaining story often shared at family gatherings and around the holiday table. I was always aware that my initial presence in this world was fraught with disappointment. I believe on some unconscious level it became my desire, my mission, to eradicate any disappointment my father may have initially felt by being the best son a man could ever have in a daughter.

Whether self-imposed or the result of some unconscious awareness of the longing my father had for a son, I had managed to make up

13

for any disappointment he may have initially felt. I wore my tomboy/daddy's girl label proudly. That label, as labels inevitably do, translated into me playing a role and I played my role well. I did everything a son would do with my father. While my sisters slept, I would get up in the wee hours of the morning to go fishing with him. I wrestled with him, just as a son would. I camped with him. I played catch. I even joined the Cub Scout Troop 670 my parents started, building my own pinewood derby car to race in troop competitions. My father had even given me the nickname of his "ace boon coon" topped off with our own special handshake. My label of daddy's girl was stuck on with crazy glue. Even the birth of my brother three and a half years later couldn't pry it off.

As with any role we may find ourselves playing, there comes a time when that role changes and the result will challenge the very essence of who you think you are. At the age of 12, my whole identity was lost in an instant. I'll never forget the moment. It was a beautiful, unseasonably warm Easter Sunday. I had just recently come to terms with wearing dresses and stood in my bedroom mirror examining my reflection and the beautiful floral patterned dress my mother had made. Within seconds, my gaze was broke by a loud crash in the bathroom. I could hear my mother calling out my father's name with no response from him. As I made it to the bathroom, I saw my father, my protector, my buddy lying lifeless on the floor. Initially, I hoped it was a prank, my father was quite the practical joker, never missing out on an opportunity to pull my leg. It soon became obvious that this was no joke. My father had suffered a massive stroke, and though not fatal, it robbed him from his ability to walk, to care for himself, and even to remember my name, his ace boon coon.

Instantaneously, at the tender age of 12, I was catapulted from my daddy's girl role and landed somewhere in the abyss of not knowing where I stood or who I was any longer. My daddy's girl label was snatched away and replaced with that of caregiver to my father. Whereas my after school activities once consisted of playing catch with my dad, they now became fill-in caregiver to my dad while my mom worked the afternoon shift. I would pick up where she left off. Along with my siblings, my responsibilities consisted of feeding my father, changing his diapers, putting him to bed and reassuring him when delusions caused by his stroke and dementia would have him out of touch with reality.

Just as I had excelled in my role as a daddy's girl, I was committed to excel in my role in caring for my father, never complaining because it was what was required of me. My teachers and friends were unaware of this new label of caregiver. After all, I was still trying to come to terms with it. As a 12 year-old, I had no idea of the repercussions that this new role of caregiver would have in my life for many years to come.

As the years progressed, I prided myself wearing my many labels and playing my roles well. Obsessively, I had to become overly competent in everything I did; mediocrity was not an option. Even in the midst of having my father become dependent on my mom and his children, I was still able to be an ideal student, excelling in academics, traveling overseas as an exchange student for a summer, graduating at the top of my class and receiving several scholarships for college. Whatever identity I lost with my father's stroke, I replaced in the academic arena. I embraced the star student role, consistently on the dean's list –even being recognized as scholar of the year during my freshman year of college. That garnered praise and recognition from my peers, which I welcomed as validation that I still mattered and had not lost myself. Then just as it had been before, my label and role of model student was challenged when in my second year of college I became pregnant.

The former daddy's girl who morphed into caregiver and was able to capture the label of scholar was now being faced with an unplanned pregnancy. Not skipping a beat, I continued with school. By this point in my life, I had played more roles than the average child star. Taking on the added role of mother just meant I would have to make room for another label and stretch my character a little more. I figured I could do it, after all that is what actors do.

Throughout my pregnancy, I continued to attend classes. I had moved from living on campus into my own home and was now commuting for over two hours a day back and forth from Detroit to Ypsilanti, Michigan. At nine months pregnant, on the very last day of the fall semester of my junior year, I went into labor on the morning of finals. I was faced with the choice of taking an incomplete grade in all of my classes or driving to the campus in labor to take my scheduled finals. I chose the latter. After all, that is what my model student role called for. I tracked down my professors, completed the four finals I had scheduled for that day, and headed directly to the hospital where I later gave birth to my first son. Two weeks later, after Christmas break, I returned to Eastern Michigan University to finish out my junior year. One year later, after taking as many as 18 credit hours a semester, I graduated from the honors college, magna cum laude. Three years later, now with the added role of wife, mother of two boys and full-time worker, I received my master's degree. Three years after that, while pregnant with my daughter, I walked across the stage and accepted my doctorate degree in psychology. The accumulation of roles didn't stop there. A year and a half after receiving my doctorate degree, I gave birth to my fourth and final child and self-published a novel.

For years, I considered this timeline of my life an impressive testament to my dedication and persistence. That was until I started my journey of transformation and realized just how pathological it was. I was playing so many roles that I was giving Sally Fields' Oscar-winning performance as Sybil a run for her money. I was living in a world where my many roles and the multitude of distractions supported a lifetime of disconnect. I distracted myself with my roles of wife, mother, sister, student, teacher, therapist and writer. Externally, it appeared I had it all together. My patients loved me, my students revered me. I could analyze you so well that you would swear I had psychic abilities. I was living an unconscious life maintained by a perpetual state of distraction. Amassing label after label reinforced my delusion of fulfillment. I had no idea at the time that what I was really seeking was a better understanding of self.

I had this seemingly perfect life, married to my high school sweetheart, four children, nice home in the suburbs, a career I loved, yet a pervasive feeling of unfulfillment was eating away at me. Years of disconnect and a repressed sense of self had reached a point where the superficiality could no longer contain itself.

There is nothing easy about choosing to strip away labels you have defined yourself by. It is so much easier and comfortable for all of us to continue to play the roles we've played for so long. But when your gut begins to subtly nudge you and eventually scream at you that unfulfillment doesn't have to be your reality and it's okay to go after what feels right, it becomes difficult to shut that noise down. Much like a schizophrenic who experiences auditory hallucinations, that inner voice won't shut up. It will demand to be heard regardless of how hard you attempt to distract yourself. My comparing this experience to a schizophrenic's experience is not in any way an attempt to be overly dramatic or mock what a person with a psychotic disorder experiences. The truth is, when you continue to live a life that lacks fulfillment and joy you invariably begin to disconnect from what is real.

As the weight of my roles began to gnaw at me, it became more difficult for me to distract myself. Transformation began to occur in every area. The changes were emotional, spiritual, as well as physical. Starting with the death of my father in 2002, eighteen years after his disabling stroke, I began to allow myself to feel. My connection with my emotions was severed when my dad became ill, and for good reason. As a young girl who had become caregiver, there was no room for what I then considered weak emotions. On the spiritual level I began to explore my connection to the world as a whole, challenging some of the religious principles that had been ingrained in me and embracing ones that seemed to fit. On a physical level, I began a diet and exercise regimen shedding the excess weight that resulted from four pregnancies. I began to feel more authentic, more balanced and more connected to myself as I faced the next major hurdle, allowing myself to get real regarding my role as a wife.

What I had learned about the role of wife came from my observation of my mother. As her understudy, I watched her every move intently, preparing for the day I would be given the opportunity to play this role. She and my dad were married on December 24, 1966 and were married 36 years before my father's death. Growing up, I would relish Christmas Eve for the obvious reason and secondly, because it was the day my parents were married. As a little girl, I created a fairy tale image of my parent's Christmas Eve wedding. Surely, their choice of this day to pledge their commitment had a level of significance that my young mind could not even begin to conceptualize. I imagined my mom coming down an aisle lined in rich red poinsettias as snow gently fell outside. Perhaps my father's tuxedo was accented in Christmas colors, or maybe he wore a green tuxedo; it was the 60s after all.

My romantic fantasy of my parents' nuptials was part of my belief system for many years until I became older and was provided with the true story behind their nuptials. As it turns out, my parents' wedding wasn't the culmination of some whirlwind courtship that had both of them smitten and wanting to seal the deal in a Christmas Eve gala. In fact, what I discovered was that my parents had only met six months prior to their wedding. My dad was visiting Detroit from his hometown of Lena, Mississippi before he was to return home to attend college on an athletic scholarship the following January. Upon meeting my mother, he was struck by her beauty. They began a summer romance and by the Fall my mother was pregnant. For my father, as for many men in that day, if you got a girl in "trouble" you did the honorable thing and married her. You, without consideration, catapulted yourself into the role of husband and father as the woman adjusted to the role of wife and mother.

Shortly after discovering they were going to be parents, they went to the courthouse to apply for a marriage license. Several dates to marry were made over the course of the next four months and missed. As my mother recalls, my father would come up with one excuse after another as to why that particular day was bad for him. He had excuses such as he didn't have bus fare to get downtown or he had to babysit for his younger cousins. Finally, on December 24th he was told by my mother that if they didn't get married on that date the marriage license would expire and they would have to come up with another $25 to re-apply. Instead of forfeiting the money and prolonging the inevitable, they caught a bus to the courthouse, married and returned to their respective homes. My father would later joke openly when retelling the story about how he contemplated ditching the ceremony by escaping from the window of the men's restroom of the courthouse, but because the courthouse was on the sixth floor, he resigned to go through with marrying my mother. My parents went on to build a loving marriage and solid home for their family.

Despite my fairytale fantasy of my parents' whirlwind courtship being shattered, I continued to rely on my observations of my mother to understand the role of a woman, mother and wife. I observed, and it became my understanding that if you enter into a relationship with someone that results in an unplanned pregnancy, you marry that person, which is exactly what I did after having my son. I never considered otherwise. As with all the other roles I was playing, I worked tirelessly to excel at my newly added roles of mother and wife. Birthdays had themes. I worked to make the holidays perfect for everyone. I committed myself to meet my husband's and children's every need, just as my mother met the needs of her family even if it compromised her own fulfillment.

Much like the role my mother played as caregiver, I became a caregiver in my marriage. I would neglect my own emotional needs to meet his. I prided myself in making things comfortable for him. I would rush home from a 12 hour day of work and school, prepare dinner and try to have all the evidence of effort put away before he made it home so he wouldn't see how much effort I put into my attempt to make things just perfect. I would figure out creative budgeting, or rob Peter to pay Paul without his knowledge because I didn't want him to worry about any financial strain. I managed the children, ran the household, organized vacations because this was my role and I wanted to make it look easy and flawless. I was the queen of distractions, distracting myself from my own discontent by engaging in perpetual doing. The children, my educational pursuits, my career, vacations, holidays, etc. all became great distractions.

Psychologically speaking, the act of distraction is a defense mechanism utilized to avoid reality and the feelings of anxiety, despondency and guilt that are bound to occur when you face the reality that things are not really as they should be. We all have, at one point in our lives, engaged in defense mechanisms, be it distraction or denial or any of the others we utilize to avoid the unpleasantness of what truly is. However, defense mechanisms should never be your primary mode of operation. They are intended to be engaged in only temporarily. When you live your life operating in denial or distraction or any of the other defense mechanisms it's just a matter of time before your psyche reaches its limit and can no longer support the heaviness of your defenses. It was at this point in my life that my defenses could no longer be supported and collided with my reality head on.

Here I was, a psychologist who prided herself in speaking on authenticity and self-actualization, whose motto was *To Thine Own Self Be True*, yet I was involved in an unfulfilling marriage. I had been with my husband since the age of fifteen long before I had any inkling of who I was. He met me at a time when I had just been snatched from my daddy's girl role and thrown into my role of a teenager stretched thin between balancing her role as honor student with the daunting role of assisting in the caregiving of her father. Unbeknownst to me at the time, I entered the relationship as an actor covered with so many labels and playing multiple roles simultaneously. My husband married the caregiver, the mother, the woman who made an art of avoiding reality through distraction. It was inevitable that eleven years into our marriage, as I began to make the conscious deliberate decision to find myself somewhere under all the debris of those labels that the quality of my marriage would decompensate.

As someone who no longer engaged in the repression of her emotions, I gave myself permission to cry, to feel, to exhibit emotions that were buried deep. As someone who would sacrifice sleep and sanity to make sure everything appeared perfect, I evolved into someone who became okay with not putting so much pressure on myself. I was changing and as each change ignited a sense of hope and excitement within me, it ignited an equal proportion of fear and confusion in my husband.

There exists a myriad of reasons as to why relationships end. There are simplified explanations ranging from "we've grown apart," to "we just couldn't see eye to eye." This simplification cannot begin to capture the infinite reasons that exist. Every situation is different with its own dynamics. Ideally, before entering into a relationship, we would have done the necessary self work of knowing oneself, but this is often times not the case. Many individuals enter into relationships as their disconnected self, operating according to roles that had been created by a lifetime of labeling.

Every relationship holds the potential to provide an increased understanding of self. Every partnership we enter into can teach you more about the character assets and flaws we possess. There exists the opportunity for reciprocal teaching and learning that can, if allowed, lead to a greater self-awareness. After nearly 20 years together and 12 years of marriage I knew the lesson was complete. The marriage no longer provided growth or positive stimulation to either of us. The longer we stayed, the more we risked initiating a state of de-compensation, despair and misery for everyone involved. As growth-seeking individuals with a natural pull toward constant evolution, a condition of non-growth leads to a bitter state of unconsciousness that has costly ramifications, including a bigger disconnect.

As my mother's understudy, my role of wife was supposed to be 'till death do us part.' No one prepared me for an alternate ending. But in my journey to rediscover and ultimately reconnect to myself, I became someone foreign to the man I married, yet someone so familiar to me. The dilemma was that the disconnected me was the person my husband was comfortable with. This is the crossroad many before me have, and many after me will arrive at. Do you grin and bear it, continue to live a disconnected, unconscious existence or do you face reality head on and allow yourself to live a life of authenticity? I knew that if I remained disconnected, I would never experience true fulfillment or authenticity, so after twelve years of marriage the curtain call came for my role as wife.

WHO ARE YOU?

"The caterpillar had no idea it was a butterfly waiting to fly until it went inside itself."

Step one in the seven steps to transformation process is aptly named *Rediscovering You* because no transformation can take place and sustain itself without you having a clear, honest understanding of self. The vast majority of the clients I have seen over the years are not individuals who are psychotic, delusional or with one step off the ledge ready to jump. Quite the contrary, the common thread in the majority of my clients over the years is a chronic state of unfulfillment. These individuals are still functioning in their daily lives, going to work, engaging in relationships, participating in events, but they express a gnawing feeling of discontent. They are still able to plant a smile on their faces, but that external smile does not truly represent what they are experiencing internally. The majority of people who come to me for help are men and women just like you and me who happen to be experiencing a sense of sadness or an unfulfilled longing for more fulfillment in life. These clients will describe a gnawing feeling of boredom, anxiety, depression, frustration that appears to be a direct result of them not living in alignment with their true nature.

My years of treating clients led me to develop a personality inventory that provides a wealth of information about the person I'm working with. To help my clients reconnect with themselves and gain insight into their true nature, each are given a brief, yet very informative, personality inventory. This inventory is printed below. Your first exercise in *Rediscovering You* is to self-administer this personality inventory. Your results serve two purposes. First, it validates that part of yourself that is begging for recognition, understanding and expression. Secondly, it reveals the damaging inconsistencies that may exist between how you present yourself to the world and what your true nature is—the self that needs to be expressed before you can grab hold to the horns of fulfillment.

WHAT BLOOM ARE YOU?

Of the four following groups, which group of words *best* describes you?

Group 1: Adventurous, Competitive, Likes Change, Entertaining, Spontaneous, Risk Taker, High Energy, Easily Bored, Persuasive, Freedom, Blunt, Variety, Stimulating, Impulsive, Hurried

Group 2: Careful, Dependable, Consistent, Traditional, Organized, Conservative, Trustworthy, Prepared, Routine, Committed, Stable, Structured, Follows Rules, Conforming, Likes to Plan

Group 3: Mindful, Deep Thinker, Self-Motivated, Analytical, Cool Under Pressure, Solitary, Knowledgeable, Tech Savvy, Perceptive, Intellectual, Questioning, Investigative, Clever, Creative, Scientific

Group 4: Loving, Kind Hearted, Open, Considerate, Artistic, Dramatic, Expressive, Intuitive, Sacrificing, Emotional, Team Player, People Person, Feeling, Lively, Accommodating

There exists four basic personality types. We all possess traits of each personality type, however, there tends to be one that best describes you. It is this dominant personality type that influences how you view and approach life. You view the world through the lenses of your particular personality type. There is no type that is better than the other. Our world benefits from all four. As an individual, it is crucial that you commit to approach life in accordance with your particular personality type. Approaching life in a manner that doesn't allow your individual personality type to shine guarantees unhappiness. Understanding and living life authentically and in alignment with your personality type is imperative to the achievement of happiness and success.

Grasping a firm understanding of your personality type provides you with a blueprint of your makeup which will ultimately serve to guide you in structuring or re-structuring the foundation of your life. Your personality in a sense is the foundation that you should build your life structure on. When you are aware and embracing of your personality type, your structure will be strong and sturdy. When your foundation consists of a lack of awareness or acceptance of self, your structure is bound to collapse in the face of difficulty.

Which of the four personality groups best describes you? For the sake of categorization, I have labeled the personality types to coincide with different flower blooms. Following is a breakdown of the four personality types and characteristics of each.

CHARACTERISTICS OF PERSONALITY TYPES

1. Wildflower	2. Mum	3. Tulip	4. Poppy
Adventurous	Dependable	Intellectual	Nurturing
Likes Change	Careful	Investigative	Artistic
Competitive	Traditional	Solitary	Open
Daring	Organized	Clever	Expressive
High Energy	Dedicated	Innovative	Intuitive
Freedom Seeking	Detailed Oriented	Philosophical	Sacrificing
Spontaneous	Committed	Self-Motivated	People Person
Charismatic	Stable	Analytical	Giving
Risk Taker	Structured	Perceptive	Accommodating
Persuasive	Loves to Plan	Cool, Calm, Collected	Affectionate

WILDFLOWERS – THE LIFE OF THE PARTY?

Wildflower personality types are often seen as the life of the party. They are adventurous by nature and desire change. Drab routine would have a wildflower type crawling out of their skin and seeking some sort of activity immediately. Wildflowers are hard wired for variety and require occasional change. They are best suited in unstructured environments where they can learn as they go. Whereas a Mum type would want to sit down and carefully read the instructions before assembling an item, a Wildflower personality would prefer to look at the picture of the assembled object and figure out what steps are required.

As children, it is not unusual for Wildflowers to be labeled the class clown, family comedian and sometimes the problem child. They are high energy and are many times erroneously labeled ADHD due to their propensity toward having many things going on in their head at one time or their inability to sit still as required in traditional school settings. Wildflower types make great entrepreneurs. They see an opportunity and will go after it with unbridled enthusiasm. They are persuasive and make ideal salespersons. They are competitive and see risk taking as par for course.

As adults, it is not unusual for Wildflowers to be labeled as irresponsible due to their tendency not to follow conventional rules. They are also labeled manipulators in light of not being opposed to bending the rules if need be. Wildflowers prefer variety over stability. They are individualists and may be accused of being selfish opportunists. They have an inborn need to experience variety and truly believe it is the spice of life.

Wildflowers are life of the party types that you may find engaging in all types of activities from rock climbing to traveling extensively and impulsively. If you call a Wildflower and suggest a spur-of-the-moment road trip, they typically jump at it. They will concern themselves with the particulars such as hotel lodgings when they arrive at their destination.

Other personality types tend to accuse Wildflowers as being irresponsible or flighty. This outgoing type does not always value being on time. Tradition or customary practices are seen as too restricting. When telling of their many adventures, Wildflowers may stretch the truth to make their story appear more exciting.

Several years ago I was seeing a client by the name of Tracey who came to me with symptoms of depression and discontent. She had married two years prior and could not understand why she was so unhappy. She loved her husband and desired to stay married to him. As we explored her personality, we discovered that prior to Tracey getting married, she was one of the most carefree and spontaneous women you could meet. Some even said she had a Bohemian quality. In her first session with me, she explained that over the last year she had an unshakable sadness and had experienced more crying spells than she cared to share. I asked her to share with me a time she could remember feeling carefree and happy. Of all things, she recalled her former Saturday morning routine of cleaning her apartment. She discussed how it wasn't the act of cleaning that made her feel good, but what she would do to make the daunting task of cleaning more pleasurable. As she continued, the memory of her happier days must have suddenly rushed in and I noticed for the first time a smile spread across her face. She discussed how she would blare her music, sing along to the lyrics using the mop handle as a makeshift microphone and slide around her freshly mopped floors a la "Risky Business" style.

"Now," she compared, "Saturday morning cleaning is such a chore. I don't even play my music anymore."

Tracey went on to share with a tinge of excitement how she used to get her hair styled in funky chic styles that always turned heads. "Now," she relented, "my styles are safe, nothing head turning about them."

As I sat facing this very conservative woman, dressed in her classic navy attire, I couldn't imagine her Tom Cruising it around her apartment or parlaying around in a trendy hairstyle. She shared how things changed once she met her husband. She was immediately attracted to this handsome, very charismatic man who was highly revered in his community. He was an aspiring politician and after attending several political events with him, she noticed that the wives of all the other political hopefuls shared similar conservative looks. In her words, she stood out like a sore thumb. In her desire not to be a political risk to her soon-to-be husband, she resigned herself to a more conservative role.

Imagine if you were my client, naturally outgoing, spontaneous and thrill seeking but you convince yourself to relinquish that part of yourself and become more structured and safe. The source behind Tracey's pervading depression was no longer a mystery to me. In her effort to force herself into a role not consistent with her nature, she became more and more disconnected. Despite her external life appearing picture perfect with the respected husband

and all the material possessions she wanted, the result of her decision to deny her true nature was an overwhelming feeling of discontent.

MUMS – THE STABILIZERS

The Mum personality type is best described as careful. They are not risk takers and thrive on structure and routine. Often inhibited in showing any part of themselves that would not be considered socially appropriate, they are easily embarrassed and disgusted by others who don't follow convention. They are sticklers for time and become easily irritated by others who are often late and don't honor commitments. They are great planners. Mums value family traditions. They appreciate doing things the way they've always been done. The saying "If it ain't broke don't fix it" would apply to a Mum type. Mums love consistency and stability. They are traditionalists and tend not to veer off the beaten path. They prefer tried and proven techniques. Mums value dependability and commitment. If they have made a commitment to a project or a person, they will see it through even if they don't find enjoyment in it. It is not uncommon for Mum personality types to remain at dead-end jobs and unfulfilling relationships simply because they've made a commitment to do so. For a Mum, it is far more admirable to remain in something, be it a relationship or job they've committed to and invested time in than to walk away. They value tradition and commitment even if it sacrifices their fulfillment.

Whereas Mums value their characteristics and see honor in their unwavering committed nature, others may view Mums as being rigid and inflexible. Because Mums have such an affinity toward tradition, they may be very critical and judgmental of people or situations that shirk tradition.

As mentioned, Mums will often times stay in relationships, jobs and friendships that no longer bring them enjoyment, for the sheer sake of honoring tradition, commitment and not wanting to implement change. They tend to place a heavy reliance on the past and the time they have invested in a person or situation. It is difficult for them to consider the opportunities that may lie ahead if it means walking away from something they consider stable. They convince themselves that stability and tradition are far more important and respectable than walking away from people or positions they've committed to. This attitude has kept many Mum personality types in unfulfilling situations.

A male Mum client of mine had been married to his college sweetheart for 24 years. For the past 10 years he and his wife had slept in separate rooms. It had been over 15 years since they had been intimate. When I broached the topic of divorce, the client looked in a state of shock that I would even suggest such a thing, "After all," he stated, "we're getting ready to celebrate our 25th wedding anniversary."

I have also encountered more than my fair share of clients whose personality results suggest they are a Mum type, but are adamant that this is not who they feel their true nature is. Upon further probing, it is sometimes revealed that the person who now scores highest in the Mum personality type was indeed hard-wired for a different personality type early on in life, but life circumstances may have forced them to adopt the Mum characteristics thus relinquishing their true nature. The same is true in instances like my client Tracey, who abandoned her carefree, eccentric personality to fit the persona of a politician's wife or as in my case, to stifle my spontaneous, creative, freedom loving nature to assist in the care of my disabled father. It is not unheard of for individuals to adopt the more structured, responsible Mum personality type as a result of life circumstances. The danger in this is that if a person does not reconnect with their true nature, a lifetime of general, gnawing discontent is guaranteed.

TULIPS – THE INNOVATORS

Tulip personality types are the problem solvers of the world. They have a thirst for knowledge and often know at least a little information about virtually every topic under the sun. The famous philosophers Socrates and Plato indeed had to be Tulip personality types. Tulips are highly analytical and enjoy breaking seemingly unsolvable problems down into small parts that will allow solutions to be fashioned. Highly theoretical, Tulip personalities are often trend setters, inventors, technicians or scientists developing innovations that change the world. Thomas Edison, Albert Einstein, and Steve Jobs were undoubtedly Tulip personality types. Tulip types value their alone time, it gives them more time to examine the complexities of whatever it is they are studying. Abhorred by incompetency, they will work to make themselves competent in whatever subject matter interests them. They tend to have an extensive vocabulary and utilize words that are not part of the realm of everyday conversation. They don't have many friends, preferring a select group of "like-minded" individuals. Socializing with people who don't share similar interests or intellect can be quite cumbersome giving them the appearance of being quite snobbish. They have the ability to remain very cool, calm and collected in most situations and are great under pressure.

Tulips tend to derive great pleasure from their work and the satisfaction they get from figuring something out or introducing a new concept to the world that will revolutionize life as we know it. When they are involved in the work of their chosen career field they can become immersed in that work, losing track of hours and sometimes days which can cause difficulty in relationships.

Denise was a Tulip friend of mine I met in my first job after college. Denise epitomized the phrase "still waters run deep." Upon meeting her for the very first time, I must admit, I didn't really like her. She came off as snobbish, didn't smile much and just seemed to have an attitude of supremacy about herself.

Whereas, there were others in the workplace that were welcoming me to the organization and bending over backwards to make me feel welcomed (no doubt these were Poppies), Denise kept her interaction with me pretty straightforward with an occasional "hello" and "goodnight." One day, a few weeks into the job, Denise noticed me reading a book that apparently she had finished reading months earlier. To my surprise, she struck up a conversation. We discovered that not only did we share a love of reading, but of writing as well. We both happened to be working on writing our first novel. The look of excitement and pure passion Denise showed while discussing the recent books she read and the characters in her novel was a stark contrast to this stoic individual that had been blowing me off for the last several weeks. A beautiful friendship was born and we have remained great friends for almost twenty years. Tulips thrive when they are able to be around individuals they consider as intellectual and passionate about their endeavors as they are. Most people don't understand the Tulips' interest in topics that most would consider boring or a far stretch from a hobby. They often feel different from most others and will be labeled antisocial by those not understanding their need for private time. When Tulips connect with other Tulips it's like a breath of fresh air.

POPPIES – THE NURTURERS

Poppy personality types are the loving nurturers of the world. Male or female, Poppy types thrive on harmony. They just want everyone to get along. They absolutely love bringing peace, beauty and love to the world. They are the peacemakers. They will work tirelessly in ensuring that everyone is happy and that they have not displeased anyone. Poppy types tend to be very affectionate and are the first to offer hugs as greetings. They make great team players and will often time downplay their own ability so as not to outshine others. Poppies are compromisers and will be the first to give in to other's wishes even if it goes against theirs. They put much value in not disappointing those around them and will sacrifice their own desires to avoid others feeling bad.

Of concern is a Poppy's tendency to be codependent, putting everyone else's need before their own, often times with devastating consequences. They are the martyrs of the world and will endure years and even a lifetime of deprivation in the name of love, family and perceived harmony. Poppies are often taken advantage of because of their giving nature. In turn, they start seeing themselves as the perpetual victim. Poppy types will spend hours discussing how they have been wronged by a person, only to turn around and reach out to that person expressing to them their undying love and devotion.

Tonya, a female client of mine who was a Poppy personality type came to me one day in tears. She had amassed a phone bill of over $1,000. When I questioned how her bill had reached such an outrageous amount in just one month's time, she explained that she had a distant relative who was in the state penitentiary. The relative had began calling her collect every night. Rather than not accept the call or be conservative about the calls she did accept, Tonya felt so sorry for her relative that she would accept each and every call and allow the cousin to talk as long as he wished. She was well aware that her phone bill was growing out of control, however, being the poppy she was, she couldn't bring herself to hurt his feelings by cutting his conversations short or limiting the calls. In addition to the phone calls, Tonya was sending her incarcerated relative money she couldn't afford to spare after he gave her sob stories about how he needed to buy basic toiletries such as soap and toothpaste, items which are free of charge to inmates. It's important to note that this relative had parents and siblings that had long before placed restrictions on his calling and cut him off financially. However, Tonya was the relative with the personality type ripe for his manipulation. Poppies tend to see the good in all and will devote themselves to a person even when all evidence suggests that the other person is manipulating the situation.

Although Poppies will often times be the victim of manipulation, they themselves can be quite the master manipulators. They will use tears and passive-aggressive techniques to get what they want. As opposed to coming right out and asking for what they desire, Poppies will use guilt trips and down right manipulation to get their desires fulfilled.

Lori was a Poppy student of mine who was shocked at the accuracy that the personality disorder depicted her. When I shared the tendency for Poppies to be manipulative, she howled in laughter and shared a story about a man she recently began dating. True to the Poppy nature, she had been spending every waking minute, either with her new beau or on the phone talking to and texting him. One Friday evening, after about two months of being basically joined at the hip, Lori's new love informed her that he had plans to go bowling with the guys. Although she dared not show it, Lori felt rejected and couldn't understand why he would prefer his friends over her. She didn't share her disappointment and pretended to be just as excited as he was about him having a night out with the guys. She sent him off with a kiss and encouraged him to enjoy every moment with his friends.

About an hour after he left, Lori proceeded to get in her car, drove unto the expressway, pulled over to the side of the road, got out of the car and let all of the air out of one of her tires. She then got on her cell phone and called her boyfriend distressed, explaining to him that she was stranded on the side of the road with a flat tire. Her boyfriend came to her rescue, cutting his night with the guys short. Lori got what she wanted and because of her boyfriend being clueless to her actions, she didn't have to be perceived as a manipulator, but a damsel in distress.

On a more serious note, over the years, I have noticed that it is the Poppy personality type, much more than any other personality type, who tends to find themselves in emotionally and physically abusive relationships. This tendency goes back to their natures of seeing the good in everyone, even when all the other evidence suggests otherwise. They have a belief that love can conquer all. Much to their friends' and family's dismay, they will remain in abusive, unhealthy relationships with them being the one paying the biggest price in the end.

Carol was a true Poppy personality type. Despite years of being abused by her husband, she maintained her belief that if she continued to show him the unconditional love he didn't receive as a child, he would one day stop the abuse and they could live happily ever after. She eventually stopped coming to sessions because she could not bear the thought of walking away from this very dangerous relationship. I ran into her years later and she appeared 20 years older than her actual age. It was apparent by her appearance that she was not caring for herself and was still engaged in this abusive relationship.

Many Poppy types will also find themselves in relationships with alcoholics and substance abusers. They may spend a lifetime hiding the fact that they are involved in a codependent relationship with a substance abuser, making excuses for their partner's behavior. In addition to the Poppy, the children involved in these relationships suffer greatly. They are part of a web of addiction that destroys their childhood and conditions them to embrace adult relationships that maintain this devastating cycle.

Poppies who are able to utilize their humanitarian traits toward rewarding endeavors can be some of the most successful and fulfilled people on the face of the earth. They must first understand their nature and protect themselves from people who want to take advantage of their qualities. Once these two requirements are fulfilled, they are ready and fully capable of making the world a truly more beautiful, loving place.

HOW YOU MAY BE INTERPRETED BY OTHERS

1. Wildflower	2. Mum	3. Tulip	4. Poppy
Selfish	Boring	Cold Hearted	Over-emotional
Manipulative	Rigid	Snobbish	Nosy
Too Flirtatious	Inhibited	Unfeeling	Gullible
Not Serious	Stuck	Isolative	Manipulative
Indecisive	Judgmental	Unappreciative	Codependent

We all are willing to own up to the characteristics of our personality that is considered positive and beneficial, but it is also important to understand how you may be interpreted by other personality types. The table listed above gives some examples of the not-so-desirable traits each bloom may appear to possess. This doesn't mean these are traits you do indeed possess. These are simply traits that others may interpret in you when you are operating according to your bloom. For example, the tendency a Mum has to follow rules and policies without question may be seen as being rigid and inflexible by other bloom types. A Mum client of mine was constantly criticized by her husband for not being willing to spend the holidays in a tropical location. She insisted that the tradition of spending Christmas at home with snow on the ground and opening up gifts around a roaring fire was not to be tampered with.

A Wildflower's social tenacity may be viewed as being too flirtatious. I once had a couple whose Mum wife always accused her Wildflower husband of flirting with waitresses when they would go out to dinner. "He even does it in front of the children," she would complain. The husband would always deny and insist he was just being friendly and outgoing which are traits that come natural to him. His friendly, outgoing characteristics were interpreted by his wife as flirtatious and disrespectful.

A Poppy who is always putting others' needs before their own feels that they are demonstrating admirable qualities. However, others, especially their loved ones, who are tired of seeing them being taken advantage of sees them as being gullible and naive. I once treated a woman who was fed up with her mother enabling her alcoholic and drug addicted relatives by always giving in to their requests for money. She would complain to her mother how her actions helped to maintain the person's addiction, however her mother insisted that she could not help being the loving nurturer for these individuals and could not bear to turn her back on them.

As a Tulip type, I remember objecting to the first personality inventory I took in my early college days that suggested I came off to others as being unappreciative. I would argue that I did indeed appreciate others and the kind things that they would do for me. I totally rejected this descriptor as false and holding no merit when it came to me. That was until I was able to view myself from another personality's perspective. I remember having a Poppy friend who had gotten me a beautiful hat and scarf set for a birthday gift. I thanked her for her gift unaware that as a Poppy bloom, a simple thank you was not enough. I didn't realize until I became more aware of the specific needs of all the personality types that a Poppy needs expressions of gratitude that go beyond a simple "thank you." So to gain a better understanding of what would have demonstrated sincere appreciation to my friend, I would observe her and other Poppy types reactions when others presented them with gifts or acts of kindness. Poppies would give huge smiles and big hugs to accompany their expression of gratitude. Some would even become overwhelmed with appreciation and eyes would fill with tears of gratitude. If I had been a Poppy type, I would have likely put the scarf and hat on right there after it had been presented to me and paraded around my dormitory for the entire day, telling everyone I encountered that this was a gift from my wonderful friend. Because I am not a Poppy, my display of appreciation fell flat in her eyes.

Years later, this same friend gave me tickets to see a Broadway play that was coming to Detroit. In an effort, and admittedly somewhat of an experiment, to see if my reaction would indeed make a difference, I showed my appreciation for her gift by giving her a big hug in addition to a slightly animated "thank you" for her gift. The look of satisfaction on her face told me immediately that my show of appreciation was in alignment with her bloom. I called her the next day to thank her once again for the tickets and told her I was really looking forward to the performance. On the day of the play, I texted the friend and told her how excited I was to be going to the performance that night. The day after the play I called her to tell her how wonderful the performance was and that her gift was indeed appreciated. My goal in demonstrating more appreciation was not to change who I am and become a chameleon to satisfy others, but to make more of an effort to meet a person where their bloom is. My knowledge of the different personality types leads me to make adjustments as necessary. We all find ourselves in situations where what comes natural to us may be regarded as offensive by others. The Tulip bloom in me would naturally think so much demonstration of appreciation would be overkill, but for my Poppy friend, going the extra mile to show my appreciation honored her bloom. We must all learn to honor each others' bloom without sacrificing our own. Allowing your bloom to flourish doesn't mean other blooms will wilt.

WHAT DOES IT ALL MEAN?

With seven billion people in the world, no two people share the same fingerprint, not even identical twins who share the exact DNA. Your particular personality bloom is just as unique as your fingerprint. You may share the same bloom as someone else, but that doesn't mean you are exactly like that person. We all possess some degree of each bloom within us. The degree to which you are influenced by all the other blooms will influence your personality makeup as well. Sure, when you meet someone whose highest ranked bloom is the same as yours, there exists an instant kinship. You two have a sort of infinite understanding; you're speaking the same language. Likewise, when you communicate and interact with someone considered to be an opposite bloom personality type, you will find that you experience more misunderstandings with that person. There will be break-downs in communication and sometimes an ongoing tug-of-war with each one of you battling to get the other person to see things from your vantage point. We've all heard the saying "opposites attract." I have discovered in my practice that this is indeed true. The problem is that although opposites may very well attract, they won't sustain in harmony unless the two opposites can learn to appreciate each other as opposed to change each other.

Over the years, the majority of couples I have counseled are ones who have opposite bloom types. A classic match-up of opposites is a Wildflower/Mum and a Poppy/Tulip. In the beginning of my practice I was absolutely amazed at how often I saw these combinations in therapy considering they are so fundamentally different. As time went on, I realized it was that fundamental difference that attracted them to each other in the first place. A Wildflower meets a Mum and is immediately impressed with their organizational skills. They marvel at how they seem to have their life in order. These are traits foreign to a Wildflower type so they are attracted to the many traits in a Mum that they themselves don't possess. A Wildflower thinks "I could use more structure and organization in my life. That Mum would be good for me."

That Mum meets that Wildflower and thinks, "Wow, look how carefree and exciting that person is. I would love to be more outgoing. This person would be great in bringing out that side of me." A relationship develops between the Wildflower and Mum and each is excited about the novelty of each other. That Wildflower spends the next several months or years, depending on how long they can maintain the charade, behaving more like a Mum. For the first time in their life they are showing up on time, picking their socks off the floor and incorporating several Mum characteristics in their life. That Mum is all of a sudden finding themselves open to engaging in some of the exciting escapades of the Wildflower. The Mum is throwing caution to the wind – approaching life uninhibited. The Mum's friends and family don't recognize them any longer and may comment how full of life or irresponsible they have become.

John and Carrie had been married for six years and was at a crossroad in their relationship. John was a true blue Wildflower. Carrie was a die-hard Mum. They discussed how exciting the first six months of their relationship had been, in fact, they married just eight months after meeting. John stated that Carrie was more fun. She would ride with him on his motorcycle, go to parties with him and spur-of-the-moment weekend trips. Now, John complained, "She doesn't want to do anything. She's a homebody and I don't want to sit at home all the time." After taking the *What Bloom are You?* personality inventory and realizing how radically different they were, I explored what attracted them to each other initially. John admitted that he was impressed at how together Carrie's life appeared to be. She had a stable job at a bank, paid her bills on time and had a way of keeping him in line. John was an entrepreneur, owned several small businesses and though he was an excellent salesman, he sucked at the organizational aspect of business. John was attracted to all the characteristics in Carrie that he did not possess and admitted that he believed she would be good in helping get his businesses in order. Instead of hiring a secretary, John took a wife. The last six years of their marriage had turned out to be less than ideal. Almost immediately, the differences that had brought them together were creating conflict in their marriage.

Angela and Phil had been dating for almost two years when I saw them for the first time. Angela was a Tulip type and Phil was a

Poppy. Initially, there was that 'opposites attract' phenomenon with Angela admiring how comfortable Phil was with showing emotion and affection, two traits on the low end of a totem pole for a Tulip type. Angela had always been criticized by family and friends for being too unemotional and unfeeling. She had a very blunt and matter-of-fact approach to relationships. Phil admired the control Angela appeared to have over her emotions, staying cool, calm and collected in crisis whereas he had a tendency to become incapacitated. He felt Angela would be great in helping him have better control over his emotions. After two years together, they, like Carrie and John, had reached a point in their relationship where they were tempted to throw in the towel. Phil had become increasingly insecure, and as Angela put it, "needy" which was leading her to become more distant and detached. As a Poppy type, Phil's thinking was if he expressed his insecurities, Angela would work to quell them. However as a Tulip type, Angela's nature was to retreat in the face of emotional insecurity. All communication between them seemed to result in one misunderstanding after another. These two were not speaking the same language, and there was no interpreter in sight. Angela would discuss how miserable she was. Friends and family loved Phil and told her she would be foolish to walk away from a man who obviously loved her so much. She stated how she had put on thirty pounds in less than a year—eating in an effort to cope with her frustration. They hadn't had sex in over a year as well. They had totally different ways of dealing with conflict and it was not only taking a toll on their relationship, but their individual emotional health.

Imagine if I told you to spend the rest of this day and tomorrow walking backwards. You could do it, but it would require consistent mental effort, deliberate focus and concentration. What I have witnessed over the years is that operating outside of your personality type is like walking backwards. You learn to navigate, take careful deliberate steps and become pretty efficient at avoiding potential stumbling blocks, but eventually and inevitably you are compelled to turn around and walk in the way that's natural for you. When you find yourself in relationships, careers or environments that are not compatible to your personality types, you may learn to compensate and function in that situation for months or even years, but eventually the constant struggle begins to tear away at you.

Now that you have uncovered your particular bloom personality type, be totally honest with yourself. Are you currently living your life in a manner that is consistent with your bloom, or are you operating outside of your true nature? Does the job you possess allow your particular bloom with its unique characteristics to flourish? Is the relationship you're in one that appreciates your individual traits or is there a constant attempt to encourage you to change and be more like another personality type? Do you feel the need to be a chameleon around your friends, never really allowing your true bloom to blossom? Are you living a life incompatible to your bloom?

If you answered yes to any of these questions, it is imperative for you to bring these areas into alignment with your personality type if you are to live a life of fulfillment and success. It doesn't necessarily mean that you have to walk away from any of these things, but you must find a way to make them consistent with your nature.

My clients are given this inventory in their very first session. It not only gives them great insight into who they are, it also validates what many have already known about themselves. The lifetime of criticism they may have received about being too emotional (Poppy), too rigid (Mum), too scattered (Wildflower), or too logical and unfeeling (Tulip) starts to make sense. They can relinquish the guilt and frustration they may feel for not being more like someone else and begin accepting themselves for who they are. They begin to realize that true fulfillment can only be acquired when they accept and operate in alignment with their true nature at all times – no exceptions. If you find yourself in a relationship, career or environment that is not consistent with your personality type and you don't want to walk away from it, you must commit to find a way to co-exist without compromising your true nature or demeaning the bloom of the person or situation that is contrary to yours.

If you are an outgoing Wildflower type in a structured job setting, explore other positions in the company that will allow you to utilize your natural abilities. If that is not possible, start exploring industries, or even more consistent with your personality, entrepreneurial possibilities that will allow your traits to flourish. If you happen to be a Mum type in a very unstructured, fast-paced work setting, explore positions within the company that are best held by structured individuals, like the bookkeeper, or human resource manager. If you are a Poppy personality type working in a very isolated job setting, explore ways that you can allow your Poppy to bloom. Offer to create a monthly newsletter, volunteer to decorate the office bulletin board, or take the initiative to plan the holiday office parties. If you are a Tulip type working in an environment that is not intellectually stimulating, refrain from finding the nearest ledge and jumping off of it to avoid all the mindless conversation. Find a local Mensa group to join to fulfill your need for intellectual stimulation.

There is no one personality type that is more dominant or more beneficial to the world. The varying personality types combined is what allows us to live in a world of diversity and newness. Would you really want to inhabit a world where everyone was exactly like you? How would the world look if there were just one type of bloom in gardens? It is the contrasts and diversity that exists among us that gives the world its spectacular beauty and stimulation.

Having now been enlightened on the different personality types and the role they not only play in the world at large, but in your individual life, you now have more of an appreciation to who you are. No longer do you need to apologize for seeing things the way you do. This is your particular bloom that is beautiful in its own right. In addition, you can no longer fault a person whose bloom may be different than yours. Understand that others have the right to bloom in their particular type as well. You can never expect that Tulip to bloom into a Poppy or that Mum to become Wildflowers. They have grown and bloomed into what they were intended to and the world is a more exciting place as a result.

THE PLANTING OF THE BLOOM - How did your personality type develop?

Now that you have gained insight into your personality type and how it plays a crucial role in every aspect of your daily living, let's explore how your personality was developed. In doing so, you can have more understanding than ever of how key events in your own personal life from childhood until your current stage in life has either enhanced your personality or led to the development of traits that may continue to be a liability in your life. Gaining insight into the formation of your personality will help you once and for all understand the factors that played a role in you becoming you. Consequently, you can gain an understanding and allow that understanding to be the fuel that propels you to enhance the traits that will be key to your success while letting go of the self-defeating, limiting traits.

After learning about their personality type, I explore with clients the eight stages in personality development as originally proposed by noted psychologist Erik Erikson. In both my personal and professional experience, I have found these stages to best parallel real life development. In each of these eight stages, especially the early stages, the potential to develop the traits that make up our personality exist. Your unique personality composite developed in response to these early stages. The development of the traits that give you power, and the ones that have no value in your quest for fulfillment can all be traced back to the state of your world in those early stages (stages 1-4). It is around the time we enter the fifth stage (Identity vs. Role Confusion) that evidence of the success or failure of the previous four stages become evident. As you read over these eight stages, ask yourself, what was the climate, circumstances and situations that surrounded your life during that time. Rely on your own remembrance or seek input from family members or friends who may recollect things you forgot or repressed.

STAGE 1- TRUST vs. MISTRUST

Let's begin by looking at the first stage of life which is approximately from birth to 18 months of age. The potential that lies in this infancy to early toddler period is the establishment of hope. As an infant, you learn to develop a sense of optimism, trust, confidence, and security if you are properly cared for and handled by caregivers during this time. When you are properly nurtured with caregivers who have the ability to care for you, provide a consistent, loving, presence you are more likely to develop optimism, trust and confidence. When your parents give consistent, adequate and nurturing care, you develop a basic trust for the world. You realize that people are dependable and the world can be a safe place. A sense of hope, confidence and optimism develops and you generally believe things will work out well in the end. If your parents or caregivers failed to provide these things, perhaps due to an absent parent or a parent who was not emotionally capable of consistent nurturing and care, you develop insecurity and a general mistrust of the world often times resulting in depression, withdrawal or even paranoia later on in life.

Probably the most poignant examples of the effects of not having a consistently nurturing presence in your life during this time of development is the countless stories that come out of orphanages that exist around the world. With far more babies than staff can handle, the relationships between adults and children are usually superficial and brief, with little continuous warmth and affection. The opportunity to connect emotionally or physically with children in the same way a physically present parent could does not exist. Children who are institutionalized at an early age without consistent continual care and nurturing often demonstrate not only delays but impairments in emotional, social, and physical development. This impairs their ability to make smooth transitions from one developmental stage to another throughout their life, having life-long consequences. In addition, I have treated countless adults who in their first years of life were removed from their parents care, often times due to alcohol/substance abuse issues or untreated mental illness. These adults tend to experience more behavior and emotional problems, such as aggression, paranoia, distrust and antisocial behavior. They also tend to have less knowledge and understanding of how to navigate in the world.

STAGE 2- AUTONOMY vs. SELF-DOUBT

The second stage occurs between 18 months and three years. The potential here is to develop an "I can do it" sense of personal will. This will is developed during this stage when you are given an opportunity to build self-esteem and autonomy as you learn new skills and are given an opportunity to practice them. During this stage, when parents guide you, praise and accept your attempt to be independent, a sense of autonomy develops in your personal make-up. The well-cared for child during this stage has a sense of confidence, pride and self-esteem that is carried well into adulthood.

If you look around at children in this stage of development their desire to exert their newfound autonomy is evidenced in their insistence on putting on their own shoes, zipping their own jacket becoming adamant about you not helping until they have exhausted all efforts to be successful at it themselves. For a child developing autonomy, they could care less that their shoes are on the wrong feet. The mere fact that they figured out how to get them on their feet is an accomplishment that they relish with beaming pride.

The parent who is too impatient to wait on the child to figure out how to get that shoe on the foot or two sides of a zipper to meet and insists on doing everything for their child at this age, their child's sense of inability and self doubt begins to pervade through their psyche, compromising their personality development.

If parents are too harsh or demanding, the child will feel defeated and experience feelings of shame and doubt. If you were not given the opportunity to practice and master your new sense of will in your environment during this stage of development, you become pervaded with a sense of vulnerability. There is a feeling of shame and low self-esteem due to your inability to learn certain skills. Your adult life thus becomes plagued with neurotic attempts to obtain feelings of control, power and competency. This may take the form of obsessive behavior such as "If I follow all rules and other's expectations exactly as I am expected then I will avoid ever feeling shame or doubt again." Individuals labeled anal retentive often had caregivers or early life circumstances that did not foster a sense of autonomy. Excessive self-doubt in childhood will result in you avoiding situations in adulthood with the belief that if you don't allow yourself to get too close to others, or take the lead in situations you can avoid the demeaning shame that will surely result if it doesn't work out.

STAGE 3- INITIATIVE vs. GUILT

The third stage is from three to five years of age. The potential here is for you to develop a sense of initiative. Often times this initiative comes out of imitating adult behavior. It is during this stage that you become curious about people and model adult caregivers. If parents are understanding and supportive of your efforts to show initiative, you develop a sense of purposeful intent, setting goals and acting in ways to reach them. If as a child you were regularly frustrated or ridiculed by your initiative, you begin experiencing guilt feelings and a decreased desire to take the initiative throughout life. These guilt feelings, when in excess, can result in inhibition and the reduced desire to take the initiative and try.

Tons of examples of a child's effort to take the initiative during this stage comes to mind. With my own children, this was the period that I would be surprised by my children with breakfast in bed, consisting of an entire box of cereal poured into a bowl, burnt toast and orange juice spilling from the glass as they made it to my room. Though, my first reaction as a parent is to cringe at the $5 box of cereal that is strewn all over the breakfast tray, I knew it was imperative not to express frustration or disdain. Crucial to their effective personality development was to praise their effort. I would offer constructive suggestions on how to avoid pouring too much cereal next time and express my appreciation for their initiative. This reinforces to the child that they can take chances, a belief that has far reaching benefits into adulthood.

I recall my oldest son Aaron taking the initiative after a trip to the grocery store to bring the grocery bags into the home. Out of the many bags he could have chosen, he, of course, chose the bag with the carton of eggs. All dozen eggs fell splat to the ground. I could have easily reinforced the look of guilt on his face with my reaction. However, knowing the importance of these stages, I did not feed into his guilt by condemning his actions. I instead offered suggestions of how to handle eggs in the future.

The most vivid example I have of a child's attempt of showing the initiative being stifled occurred while on a field trip to a nature center with my son's preschool class. There was a little girl name Sherry who seemed to take a liking to me. It was common knowledge that Sherry's mother was not present in her life due to drug addiction. Sherry's chaperone during this trip was her grandmother who was also her legal guardian. Her grandmother presented as irritated and short-fused, likely out of frustration that she, in the golden years of her life, had to take on the role of childrearing again. Throughout the trip, I would catch Sherry watching my son and me interact. She would be smiling as if she was vicariously experiencing the undivided attention that a mother can provide. I would smile back at Sherry and wave and she would shyly return the gesture. Half-way through the trip, while on a nature walk, that shy little girl mustered up enough courage to walk over to me and say hello. She asked me a question about the name of the tree we were observing and before I could even get my response out, her grandmother began berating the little girl. She angrily told Sherry to leave me alone and get away from me. She rounded out her scolding by telling Sherry that no one wanted to be bothered with her. In just those few seconds I watched any courage, initiative and confidence that may have developed in Sherry's short, troubled life being sucked right out of her.

STAGE 4 - INDUSTRY vs. INFERIORITY

Stage four occurs roughly from six to 12 years of age. The potential here is to develop a sense of industry and competency. We learn so much during this stage. We become creative and have the potential to accomplish numerous new skills and knowledge. As our world begins to expand through our school and neighborhood, we develop social contacts outside of our family unit and begin connecting with peer groups. We start to discover our own personal talents and what sets us apart from others. Perhaps it's our athletic ability, or natural aptitude toward math, creative writing, singing, etc. If caregivers support your industrious efforts, a sense of competency develops. If caretakers do not support the child, feelings of inferiority are likely to develop. It's during this very social stage you may begin to experience feelings of inadequacy and inferiority among your peers. If these feelings are not resolved through development of your own sense of ability or aptitude at something, you are left with serious deficits in your competency in life leading to a sense of inferiority, inertia, and underachievement.

Margaret was a student in my introductory psychology class. Not a typical student, she was in her early 50s and returning to school after 32 years in the workforce. After discussing these stages in class, Margaret waited patiently after class to speak to me. With tears in her eyes, she shared with me how much my lecture resonated with her. She indicated that she had a 12 year- old son at home that she had become increasingly concerned about over the past few years. Crying by this time, she indicated that she had always been told that she would never have children. Much to her surprise, in her early 40s, she became pregnant. The birth of her son was a blessing she never expected. He quickly became her top priority and she protected him at all costs.

In her son's infancy, Margaret saw to it that he was provided with a safe, nurturing environment. She met and exceeded his every need. Her role as a parent and primary caregiver at this time allowed her son to develop a sense of trust in his environment. The problem began as her son began to move into his toddler and school-age years. As would be expected, he started exhibiting the desire for more autonomy and independence. He wanted to walk up and down stairs unassisted and put on his own clothing.

Margaret admitted that it was around this time that her over protectiveness toward him developed. She was terrified at the thought of her son hurting himself in some of his autonomous pursuits. He was the child she never thought she would have and she was committed at all costs to see to it that he was protected. She admitted that more often than not she, out of fear, would stifle his independence. For Margaret, a skinned knee or bruised arm was an indication of her neglect toward providing a safe environment for her son. She failed to understand that her son's autonomous pursuits, even the ones that may lead to failure, were crucial to his healthy development.

As her son grew older and moved into other developmental stages without successfully achieving the previous ones, his attempts to master his current stage was futile. He lacked the opportunity to take the initiative and discover his competency in various areas. As the world became a bigger place for him with more opportunity for experiences, Margaret's fears and protectiveness grew exponentially. By the time Margaret landed in my lecture hall, her 12 year- old son was struggling terribly with low self-esteem and lack of confidence. With tears streaming down her face, Margaret explained how her son was not fitting in with his peers. He didn't possess the confidence to seek out friendships or try out for teams or go to camps, or engage in any of the activities typical children his age pursued. She stated, regretfully, that during my lecture on the eight stages of personality development, a light bulb went off and she realized that she did more harm than good to her son's development. Inconsolable by this time, I assured Margaret that all was not lost and although ideally her son should have developed a healthy sense of autonomy and initiative in earlier stages, it wasn't too late for him to start engaging in the behaviors that would help him develop the traits she desired for him.

It was crucial that before Margaret's son moved into the next stage of development (identity vs. role confusion) that he grabbed hold of the key developmental traits that had eluded him due to his mother's interference. Not to do so would prove disastrous in his future as the next stage would mark the first stage in which our development depends primarily on our own actions.

STAGE 5- IDENTITY vs. ROLE CONFUSION

Stage five plays out from ages 12 to 18. Young adults attempt to develop identities and ideas about strengths, weaknesses, goals, occupations, sexual identity and gender roles. Teens "try on" different identities. Identity crisis run rampant during this stage which is actually a good thing. This is indeed the stage to explore what fits and what doesn't fit, what feels good and what doesn't. The potential in this stage is to develop a sense of commitment to your individual identity and to foster a sense of belongingness with others, often outside of our family unit, who share similarities. We begin sustaining loyalties and learn that we can be friends with very different people.

Prior to stage five, our development was largely influenced by what was done to us by our caregivers. It is at this point that our development begins to depend a great deal on our own efforts to progress during the stages. This is the period in which we struggle to find our own identity while struggling with societal pressures of "fitting in" to whatever our specific environment deems right or wrong. It is during this stage that we begin to develop a strong affiliation and devotion to ideas, causes and friends. A sense of belongingness is a human need. We all possess an inherent need to feel connected to others. This need is magnified in this stage of development as the group you choose to affiliate with plays a key role in your sense of identity. During this stage, adolescents will find themselves shedding friendships established in earlier stages and begin acquiring affiliations with people and groups that they feel an affiliation toward.

We begin to seek out friends and groups that will help to solidify the identity we are forming about ourselves. These friends and groups begin to form our surrogate family and we spend considerable time interacting with our surrogate family. For some adolescents, the affiliation may be with gangs, cults or incorrigible peers. For others it may be school organizations, sports teams, etc. The nature of the group chosen will depend a great deal on the success or lack thereof of the previous stages. It was during this stage of development that my father became ill. Despite my healthy development throughout the stages until this point, the crisis of my father's illness affected my formation of a solid identity. My identity became tied to my roles which had lasting ramifications.

Lisa was in this stage of development when she became pregnant at the age of fourteen. She hid the pregnancy well into her second trimester and by the time her parents discovered it, she was already six months pregnant. She gave birth to a healthy baby girl on her fifteenth birthday. Fast forward eighteen years and Lisa showed up in my office, a 33 year-old mother of an eighteen year-old daughter who was getting ready to begin her first year of college. Lisa sat before me wrestling with a flood of emotions and difficulties. She expressed her disappointment regarding years of unhealthy intimate relationships and her desire for fulfillment in life. She admitted to feeling an overwhelming sense of regret and even jealousy as she watched her daughter embrace the college life that she was never able to experience. She discussed how she had always desired to go into the medical field and perhaps pursue becoming a neurologist as the human brain always fascinated her. Now in her early 30s she was filled with confusion of what her next move in life would be. When Lisa became a teenage mother during this stage, role confusion occurred. Though chronologically, she was well past the 12-18 year-old age range for this stage, developmentally she had never progressed past this stage in a healthy manner.

Despite the tendency some may take to minimize the importance of developing an identity during this stage, identity development can't be ignored. This stage can't be skipped if you are to live a fulfilled life. Role confusion may occur due to circumstances and identity formation may lay dormant, but when you least expect it, whether you are a 55 year-old man, 70 year-old retiree or as Lisa discovered, a 33 year-old mother of a high school graduate, your true identity will beg for expression.

Stage 6- INTIMACY vs. ISOLATION

Stage six occurs from age 18 to 35. The potential exists here to give and receive love by developing intimacy with others. During this stage, you begin to seek companionship and love. You develop the ability to be close, loving and vulnerable with romances and friendships. Successful progression in the previous stages equips you with a love and appreciation of self. Thus, you are able to give love and appreciation to others. Most will "settle down" and start families during this time. If you have not successfully achieved key features in earlier stages of development, the risk exists for you to become isolative or to forge relationships with individuals who are themselves incapable of true intimacy and love. You may find yourself in relationships, marriages and friendships that are not fulfilling. It's virtually impossible to make healthy relationships and friendship selections when you have not properly achieved the previous developmental stages. If your early life circumstances have resulted in you evolving into an adult with a natural distrust of others, someone lacking the confidence to take the initiative, and still struggling to establish a firm identity, you will inevitably attract relationships that reflect the same.

STAGE 7- GENERATIVITY vs. STAGNATION

The seventh stage occurs during the largest span of our life, from age 35 to 65. The desire here is to be actively engaged in a life that is personally meaningful. Others desire to take it one step further and involve themselves in pursuits that leave a lasting mark on the world. We take on more responsibility than ever during this period and countless life shifts can occur from children being born, to children leaving home, changes in career, marriage, divorce, etc. We want families and careers that are fulfilling and desperately want to grab hold of that American Dream promised to us. Those with a strong sense of purpose with healthy outlets to engage in that purpose will develop a sense of accomplishment with the desire to help the next generation to do the same. When you are progressing through this stage in a healthy manner, you will find yourself contributing to society whether it be through work, family, philanthropic or volunteer work or just by being an all around good person.

It is inherent to desire being a contributing member of society. Inactivity and meaninglessness in this stage can result in depression, anxiety and that proverbial mid-life crisis. If a person fails to establish a sense of generativity they may feel purposeless and stagnated in life. The feeling of being stuck may result in that person being stingy and self-absorbed. As a result, they offer very little to others and fail to recognize any sense of meaning in life.

In recent years, countless people who once considered themselves purposeful and contributing found themselves in a state of unexpected stagnation. The economic collapse of the recession affected many, who never imagined they would be faced with such economic ruin. Loss of employment, home foreclosure, depletion of savings would send even the most generative individual in a downward spiral overwhelmed with despair.

As a college professor in the Metropolitan Detroit area (one of the hardest hit areas in the U.S. during this time) my classes became flooded with these casualties of the recession— individuals who were well into middle-age entering college to pursue career changes. My practice also saw an increase in individuals seeking therapy in an attempt to cope with the major life changes economic collapse brings. It soon became apparent that individuals who had progressed more effectively in the previous stages of development fared far better in dealing with this major life change. They tended to view themselves as still having some degree of control over their lives while the individuals who struggled through previous stages of development tended to regard themselves as powerless victims. They believed they possessed little, if any, control over turning things around for themselves and becoming generative adults once again. The stagnated individuals ruminated regularly over the laundry list of items they lost in the recession. These casualties would inject in every conversation how the external forces of the recession had ruined their lives. Their sense of helplessness and victimization had them stagnated, unable to grasp onto any new opportunities that may exist for them.

Sean was in his late thirties when he lost his job with the automotive industry. Growing up, his expectation was to work for one of the Big Three automotive companies, make a good living and retire after thirty-five years. This is the path his father, grandfather and many of his relatives followed. He started working in the industry just out of high school and as planned was making a good living and supporting his family until the economic collapse. Losing his job of nearly 20 years left Sean struggling with feelings of role confusion and stagnation. After attending a workshop I conducted, Sean contacted me to begin therapy sessions. He shared with me the difficult time he was having as he felt totally lost and displaced with no inkling of what direction to head in. He had always identified himself as a worker in this industry. He considered himself to be productive and purposeful in his work. Now there was no work to connect to. His feeling of stagnation was affecting every facet of his life including his marriage. He expressed that he had lost all motivation and spent most of his day watching television, admitted to drinking more and had not been intimate with his wife in nearly a year. The next several months was spent helping Sean to explore and establish an identity that would be firmly rooted in the true essence of who he was, not what he did for a living—an identity that would remain generative with a sense of purpose even when life throws him a curve ball.

STAGE 8- INTEGRITY vs. DESPAIR

The eighth and final stage occurs between age 65 until death. During this stage, you have the potential to recognize and share a profound sense of wisdom or an overwhelming sense of despair as it pertains to the life you have lived. This is a time of great reflection involving evaluating the successes and failures in your life as well as accepting your aging and mortality. Reflection during this stage will either result in a sense of integrity—that is contentment, feeling as though you have led a meaningful life, took chances and were a valuable contribution to society, or a sense of despair, ruminating over a life plagued with failures and a lack of satisfaction. As they get closer to the end of their lives, those in despair may recognize it's too late to right what they perceive as their many failures and may develop a disdain toward life. Their conversation may be plagued with bitterness and negativity. The grumpy old man syndrome, which can apply to both men and women, is often recognized in this stage. As further evidence of the unfortunate tendency toward despair many have in this stage, recent studies reveal that senior citizens have one of the fastest growing rates of depression and suicide among age groups.

Sara was an eighty year-old woman currently residing in an assisted living facility when I evaluated her at the request of her family for a guardianship hearing. According to her children, Sara had a tumultuous relationship with most people throughout her life, including her family. Described by her family as a bitter, resentful old woman, her children admitted to not visiting her often and not bringing her to family functions due to her cantankerous disposition. When I evaluated Sara, it soon became obvious that she was wrought with a myriad of emotions ranging from anger, guilt, resentment and despair. Sara was adamant to share with me, as much as she could in a two hour evaluation, the lifetime of unfairness that had been dealt to her and the lack of regard she felt she received from her family. She would often interject in her rumination that if she could go back and do things over she would.

There are indeed countless Saras that exist in the world— individuals who will find themselves in golden years that aren't so golden. One of the questions I ask my clients when counseling them is, "Are you currently living a life that will give you a sense of integrity and fulfillment in your later years?"

Consider your own life against these stages. In the following table, indicate under *Significant Life Events*, any significant life events that occurred during that stage. If there are none you can recall, either from memory or reports from family members, simply leave that area blank. In the final column under *How Has It Affected You* indicate how you feel the significant life events affected your personality development.

Developmental Stage	Significant Life Events During This Developmental Stage	How Has It Affected Personality Development
Trust vs. Mistrust birth-18 months		
Autonomy vs. Shame and Doubt 18 months - 3 years		
Initiative vs. Guilt 3 years - 6 years		
Industry vs. Inferiority 6 years -12 years		
Identity vs. Role Confusion 12 years - 18 years		
Intimacy vs. Isolation 18 years - 35 years		
Generativity vs. Stagnation 35 years - 65 years		

Integrity vs. Despair 65 years - beyond		

Now that you have explored your own personality development in each individual stage, answer the following questions:

Is there any particular stage that stands out for you?

What stage, if any, did the most traumatic event occur?

Which of these stages do you feel you did not progress through as successfully as you would have preferred?

What can you do now to achieve the healthy developmental milestones (trust, autonomy, initiative, industry, identity, intimacy, generativity, integrity) that are crucial to your success and fulfillment in life?

CHAPTER TWO

STEP 2: C.A.L.M.S. -- LIVING IN THE NOW

"We are becoming more consciously aware, this return to our natural state of being will be the saving grace of humanity."

~ Dr. Rose Moten

Have you ever watched a child playing, perhaps laying in the grass, captivated by the clouds in the sky as they indiscriminately moved in and out of some recognizable shape? Have you ever witnessed children losing themselves in play, emanating the sweetest laughter that can only be described as pure, unadulterated bliss? Or perhaps you can remember a time in your life when you have been totally immersed in a joyful moment, fully conscious and fully aware. We all have experienced these moments, yet as we move through childhood, adolescence and into adulthood these moments become far and few in between.

As human beings, just as with every other species of animal on the face of this earth, it is our natural state of being to be fully present and consciously aware in each and every moment. Our conscious awareness is what ultimately connects us to the universe. It is through this connection to the universe, through our conscious awareness and living in the now, that we find and restore our balance. Conscious awareness, or living in the now simply put can be described as a state of uninterrupted being; a state of feeling totally connected to life. That connection is to the present moment. A more metaphysical explanation of conscious awareness would entail me considering conscious awareness as the highest level of non-judgmental, pure love existence you could experience. Some choose to explain it as tapping into God consciousness. Whichever explanation you choose to embrace, understand that conscious awareness is our natural state of being. Yet we have abandoned it by the wayside. Somewhere along the line, something went terribly wrong. We went from existing in a very consciously aware state of being (living in the now), to an unconsciously aware state of doings (constant, pathological thinking that never seems to shut off). It is this constant thinking and unconscious awareness that we operate in that has become the culprit behind the chronic state of unhappiness, despair, depression and anxiety. We transformed from a state of human beings to human doings with the *doing* being never-ending, pathological thinking.

You may be saying to yourself that this is a pretty strong accusation to make about the act of thinking, especially when most of us have become convinced that it is thinking that maintains our existence. Most of us are familiar with René Descartes famous quote, "I think, therefore I am." In Eckhart Tolle's powerful book, *The Power of Now*, Tolle states that this philosophical statement of Descartes was one of the most detrimental statements ever made by man. Our existence was based on and evolved out of pure consciousness. We were born and intended to be conscious beings. Conscious awareness is how we plug into the infinite knowledge and restorative power of the universe. The act of thinking was intended to be a just a minute portion of our consciousness. Thinking was intended to be nothing more than a simple tool utilized for practical purposes such as planning or to create strategy. However, the scales somewhere along the line were tipped. It has taken over our conscious awareness much like a malignant tumor takes over healthy cells. Purposeless, constant thinking managed to push conscious awareness out of the way and the results have been devastating. We now identify ourselves through our thinking. To paraphrase Descartes, we think, therefore, we are.

Our inability to live in the now is due primarily to our inability to turn off the incessant thinking we engage in for the majority of our waking hours. Not only is the majority of our daily thought usually pointless, without any end goal, but it is extremely damaging to our emotional and physical well being. Thinking that is not conducted for the purpose of strategy or planning, does not connect us to the universe. It is not restorative, nor does it provide us with the sense of balance we need to be successful in the world. The pathological constant mind chatter of the thinking we tend to engage in throughout the majority of our day connects us to the past and the future. Past and future are two elements that don't exist. They are simply culprits that rob us of the now and keep us connected to crisis and conflict. We re-live the crisis of the past through our thinking, whether that be the crisis or trauma of some event that happened 20 years or 20 minutes ago. Our minds have become a never-ending movie that can take us precisely back to a point in the past and like a broken record we will replay that scene over and over again. This monstrous purposeless thinking that has taken over our being has become so sophisticated that it also creates never-released movies in our mind. Images of scenes that we have not personally experienced will pervade our daily existence and we create a myriad of *"what if"* scenarios ranging from wishful thinking to downright horrifying possibilities.

Early on in my practice, it became pretty obvious that pathological thinking was maintaining most of the *dis*-ease my clients presented with. I didn't initially recognize thinking as the issue, mainly because I personally identified with pathological thinking and could not shut it off. I, like most people, regarded constant thinking about my past or my future as my default setting. The disconnect from being a conscious human being begins to occur during our childhood. For most, it's a gradual occurrence influenced by the demands, beliefs and fears of our family and the world as a whole. For others, the disconnect can occur more dramatically, as the result of some traumatic experience that leads you to want to run from your present moment. Any child that experiences a traumatic event, especially an event that is going to be experienced repeatedly like physical/sexual abuse, neglect, extreme poverty, etc., will understandably want to escape their present moment. Who wants to live in constant awareness when that awareness is so devastating? Research has long proven that disorders such as dissociative identity disorder, better known as multiple or split personality disorder, are most likely triggered by traumatic events. In an effort to cope, the child learns to escape from conscious reality and instead opts for an existence in which they themselves don't have to participate in. Less dramatic and more common is the tendency for us early on in life to learn to disconnect from our present moment by identifying with the past or future through our thinking. This is where thinking becomes less about strategy and planning and more about escape. The door to the *dis*-ease of thinking is opened at this point, never to be closed again for many. Thinking has now been given open access to our being and begins to push our awareness out of awareness.

As a young girl living with a father's chronic illness, there was no part of me that relished being consciously aware. For me, conscious awareness was nothing more than a constant, nagging reminder of the unfairness that had been dealt to my family. There was no part of me that wanted any part of the now. I was a 12 year-old girl whose daily responsibilities included caring for her father as a mother would care for a child. I dealt with the changing of the diapers, feedings and delusions that were part of the dementia by no longer identifying with my present moment. I engrossed myself by remembering the past I once had with my dad, the boat rides, the fishing trips, the joking around. The good old days, when my dad was well and my family would give a Norman Rockwell painting a run for its money. I grabbed on to a past that was a lot more pleasant than the present and anxiously hoped for a future that would include my father becoming well again. As the years passed and it became apparent that my dad would not get better, my focus shifted from ruminating on the past to becoming obsessed with creating a better future for myself. I took on what I like to call a microwave mentality. Everything that I needed to do to create a better future needed to be done yesterday. Watching a 36 year-old man wiped out by illness has a way of making you believe that you don't have the luxury of patience. My thinking was that at any moment, my life could be cut short too, so I had to get everything in quick, fast and in a hurry. This exponentially increased my unconscious living. I continued to live this way over the next 20 years, giving no value to living in the now. I couldn't sit still, I had to be in perpetual motion and future-focused because not doing so would force me to attend to the now and the now was not an awareness that appealed to me.

Choosing not to live in the moment and be consciously aware is not just pointless and useless, it is quite dangerous and destructive as well. The first clue that my unconscious living was wreaking havoc in my life was at the age of 24 when I began experiencing heart palpitations. I had episodes of irregular heart beats that would go on for days at a time. I eventually went to a cardiologist who had me wear a heart monitor for a week so the irregularity could be recorded. One doctor diagnosed mitral valve prolapse; another's diagnosis was inconclusive. Ironically, this experience didn't convince me to slow down, it had the opposite effect. Though the cause of the palpitations turned out not to be as severe as feared and the palpitations appeared to be more stress related, the thought of me having some serious medical impairment reinforced my disconnect from the now. In my pathological thinking, the non-promise of tomorrow meant I needed to work even harder today. I continued to burn the candle from both ends, placing more and more responsibility on myself. Over the next seven years, I racked up two more degrees and three more children all while working full-time and starting a business. I was, like so many others are today, trapped and enslaved by pathological unconscious living.

THERE'S NO FUTURE IN YOUR PAST

During a television interview George Burns, at the age of 100 was asked, "How do you keep going?" His response, "I always look forward. I never look back." The Bible shares the classic story about Sodom and Gomorrah. Lot and his family were told to escape for their life and "look not behind thee lest thou be consumed." Most of us know where the story went from there. Lot's wife couldn't resist looking back at the devastation behind her and subsequently she turned into a pillar of salt. In modern day, the pathological "looking back" has consumed our spirits. Many convince themselves that the past was the best years of their life or their past was so horrendous that there is no way they could ever rise above it. Either belief robs a person of the magnificence of the presence. Past-focused thinking has contributed to massive statistics in depression. Being past-focused burdens us, it makes us stagnant and prevents us from moving forward. Most of us have managed to create a world for ourselves where living in the moment has gone from being our natural set-point to a virtual impossibility.

We live in a world today where at any given moment, most people are either thinking compulsively about the past or anxiously about the future. We have taken this wonderful gift of purposeful thought and transformed it into a monster. The tail is now wagging the dog. When you are engaged in compulsive, pathological thinking, it is impossible to be conscious and conscious awareness is our natural state of being. Our waking hours have become consumed with never-ending thoughts about our past or thoughts about our future. When we become consumed with past and future-focused thinking, we rob ourselves of the potential that exists in the present, in the here and now. Bottom line is, there is no future in your past and there is no past in your future. The past has no bearing on the present, other than the power you give it to affect your life.

Many have convinced themselves that their past was so horrendous that any chance of true peace and serenity is something not to expect in their lifetime. They continue to pull evidence from the past of why their present should not be one of enjoyment. For many of these people they can get to the point in life where they almost seem to find pleasure providing reason after reason of why they should be depressed. They relive their past by telling their story over and over again, not in an effort to share their triumph over their traumas, but to provide continued evidence of their right to be depressed, dejected and disillusioned. So the past becomes a crutch, it becomes a welcomed handicap for the individual, an excuse of why they can't progress. Waking thoughts and daily conversations are consumed with the memories of when they were indeed a victim or when they were ridiculed or impoverished or abused or abandoned. Though the offenses may have occurred years, even decades ago, emotions have memories and the intensity of the pain that was experienced in the past can actually be experienced to the same degree now, thus keeping you tethered to your past.

For many who engage in the re-living of their past through their thoughts and/or retelling of their story, the thought of not being able to tell or think about their tragic story over and over again is frightening. Many of my depressed clients over the years actually found it reinforcing to ruminate on their past and how they've been wronged. Surprisingly, they would often demonstrate some resistance when I attempted to implement strategies to break their unhealthy connection to their past. This is because after years of identifying with their story, they begin to believe a departure from it would leave them without an identity.

The only value the past holds is that of understanding. We understand ourselves by delving into our past; we find ourselves by coming into the present, the now. There comes a time in all of our lives where we must decide if we are going to be an echo of our past or glory of the now. At any given moment we are making the choice to carry the past with all of its pain, longing and sorrow on our shoulders or release it and embrace the power of the now. My passion and desire is for people to live a liberated life. Throughout history we have celebrated the freedom that people experience after liberating themselves from some horrendous oppression—women's liberation, liberation from racial inequities. As we settle into the 21st century, the liberation that will have the biggest impact on our evolution and our survival will be the liberation from our faulty thinking. One common denominator I have discovered in people who are able to truly transform their lives exponentially are those who are willing to challenge what they have come to know as truth.

The Whentality

Just as a preoccupation with the past creates depression, an overreliance on the future creates anxiety. Many have adopted an *"I'll be happy when"* mentality, which I like to call a *Whentality*.

*"I'll be happy **when** I find the man/woman of my dreams."*

*"I'll be able to relax **when** all my bills are paid."*

*"I'll be able to breathe **when** I find another job."*

This whentality is problematic in many ways. First, "***when***" never seems to come. *When* becomes the dog chasing its tail, like the sign posted at bars that reads "Free beer tomorrow." Show up tomorrow and the sign reads the same. You will never be able to collect on that free beer.

This future-focused existence robs us of the magic of the day. Many in modern-day western society have conditioned themselves to believe that they must wait until some opportune time in the future before they can truly live. For some, that time may be the weekend or when the kids leave home or when they finally get that dream job. There is an expectation that these "*whens*" we've deemed as our salvation will roll in like pomp and circumstance and make everything right. Inevitably, when these much anticipated "*whens*" occur without any radical shift in our perceived sense of fulfillment, we are forced to consider that maybe our serenity was not to be found in the future. It can only be found now, in the present, in our conscious awareness. Happiness will always elude you if you turn it into a goal. You've got to find it in this moment.

It is indeed our natural state of being to remain conscious. Thinking and conscious awareness are incompatible. They can't co-exist, however the dependency we've created in pathological thought creates the despair so many experience on a daily basis. It is indeed a dependency. Just as a dependency to alcohol, cocaine, prescription drugs or any other substance, you no longer feel you can stop your constant thinking. It has taken over you.

Confusion comes forth when we are considering too many things at one time, when we are not conscious and in the moment. Clarity comes forth when we are conscious and learn to increasingly remain singular in thought. It was never intended for our minds to be consumed with so many unnecessary, bombarding thoughts. Our minds have become a battlefield and thinking is the enemy that we just can't seem to conquer. As a response to my and the majority of my clients' battle with pathological thinking, I created the C.A.L.M.S. approach. C.A.L.M.S. stands for Conscious Awareness Leading to the Manifestation of Success. All the research, contemporary as well as classic literary works, consistently asserted that true life success could only be manifested by those who learn to live consciously aware. The C.A.L.M.S. approach challenges clients to increasingly engage in more conscious awareness as they eliminate pathological thinking which would ultimately restore them to a state of balance. C.A.L.M.S. consist of the following exercises which will be discussed on the following pages: Challenging What You Know, Reframing, Eliminating Faulty Beliefs and Engaging in Conscious Activities. C.A.L.M.S. provides you with the necessary tools and with the right tools, anything is possible.

CHALLENGE WHAT YOU KNOW

Most people are what psychologists call cognitive misers. Cognitive misers are people who prefer not to incorporate any new thought patterns in their lives. Instead, they recycle the same beliefs, truisms and mindsets that have been ingrained in them from their childhood. Any situations they encounter that are contrary to their particular beliefs are immediately regarded as untrue and discarded. On average, most people choose not to disrupt the long regarded belief system they have come to know and embrace.

The personal truths that many of my clients over the years considered to be gospel ranged from such beliefs as: every man cheats, money is the root of all evil, happiness and salvation are only obtainable after you die and go to heaven have impeded the progress of many of my clients. Upon challenging their beliefs, many find themselves initially wrought with guilt and even a tinge of betrayal to consider the possibility that some of their long-held beliefs, many of which were passed down by parents and other family members, may not hold relevance or value in their lives as an adult.

In addition to our thoughts, our beliefs also keep us tied to the past. It may be our belief that the past was horrendous or the past was the best part of our lives. We hold on to beliefs for one of two reasons: either those beliefs were so ingrained and conditioned within us that to deviate from them would be like cutting off a limb or, over time, our experiences have reinforced those limiting beliefs. Challenging what you know involves reconfiguring your belief system. This is no easy task considering we may have lived a significant part of our lives witnessing those beliefs being reinforced. Our beliefs influence our behavior and once we have those beliefs established there is not much effort put into challenging them.

So many people fail to ever experience a place of personal fulfillment in their life because of the intense fear they feel in having to place all of the beliefs under a microscope, and having to honestly decide what goes and what stays. For many, this task is so difficult because they have become accustomed to living a life as a cognitive miser, maintaining thoughts wrought with mediocrity, strife and low expectations. These individuals have established a belief set point that doesn't allow for transformation. Far too many people have found comfort in chaos and familiarity in a life of complacency. They may freak out if you mention change because change will require them to look at the world through new lenses. The fear of the unknown for some is far more powerful than the hope of what could be.

Throughout my years as a psychologist, I have noticed that the clients who make the most radical changes in their lives and execute extraordinary transformations are the ones willing to honestly challenge every value, belief system and truth they've come to know. By no means does this suggest you discard every prior belief you've held true. It is to say, however, that you begin to take an honest, open evaluation of the thoughts, beliefs and practices that may be stifling your growth. Transformation, by definition, requires dramatic change in both your behavior and thoughts.

REFRAMING

One technique I use with my clients is a process called *Reframing*. Reframing explores the origins of our limiting beliefs that have been inherited from our families, communities and/or culture. The purpose of this exploration is to gain a better understanding of where and whom they originated from which ultimately gives you the courage to challenge those beliefs. Most limiting beliefs originate from either limited knowledge or false information. There was a time people believed the world was flat, but new information that resulted from exploration challenged that, and now it is universally accepted that the world is round. Imagine if there still existed a segment in the population who refused to incorporate this new knowledge into their belief system. They wouldn't travel great distances for fear of falling off.

For many, limiting beliefs originated from real threats that existed at some point in time. For example, for the majority of blacks during slavery and the civil rights era it would have proved detrimental to befriend or trust someone outside of your race. Yes, at that point in time it was a real threat and in that person's best interest to establish that as a belief system. Fast forward nearly 150 years and I still encounter individuals who are adamant about not opening up or trusting others based solely on their racial makeup, without any real, current personal evidence to support their belief.

I have worked with countless clients who find themselves struggling between maintaining their long-held beliefs with their desire to embrace attitudes and behaviors that are contrary to what they have always considered true. In their quest toward transformation it was necessary for them to challenge many of the beliefs, rules and standards they once held as their absolute truth. Many clients would come to realize that some of their ingrained beliefs were not only liabilities, but the largest obstacles standing between them and their life of success and fulfillment.

Karen, a former client revealed to me that as a child, she was told by her parents not to expect a great or happy life. They told her that the lifestyles she saw on television or observed in some of the more prestigious neighborhoods in town was not in the cards for people like them. Karen's belief set-point was a life where she dared not want or expect anything more than mediocrity. She was convinced that dissatisfaction and unfulfillment was her destiny. Consequently, she went from one unfulfilling relationship, job and living environment to the next. She did not believe she was deserving of more. Within a year of beginning life coaching with me, she was working in a career that she loved and living in a beautiful home in a part of town that she never believed she could live.

Edmund was the child of parents who worked as sharecroppers in the south before migrating to the north to work in the automotive industry. His parents believed in the value of laborious work. He was told by his parents that education was a waste of time. Despite his burning desire to study law he never pursued college because of the high regard he held toward his parents' opinion. He worked more than twenty-five years in manual labor positions, often times immersing himself in law books during his thirty minute lunch breaks. In his late forties, he finally gathered the courage to challenge his parents' view on education and enrolled in his first college course with the intent to eventually go to law school.

Melissa, a 29 year-old coaching client shared with a close friend her desire to write a book. Her friend responded that writing a book was a stupid idea. Melissa suppressed this desire for nearly five years, never bringing up the topic of writing a book to anyone again until she made the commitment to challenge her limiting beliefs. Two years later she self-published her first novel. She is currently working on her third book and has quite an impressive following.

I had been seeing Shauna in therapy for several months when she declared with a sense of hopeless defeat, "I'm sick of always doing the right thing and never getting ahead." I responded, "Have you considered that maybe the right things that you are doing are not the right things for you?" She gave a puzzled look, not really knowing how to respond. I went on to elaborate that one of the biggest mistakes we make in life is to live by a set of prescribed rules that are not compatible to our nature or to live by the same rules our parents lived by; either choice guarantees discontent.

"If in the last few years you haven't discarded a major opinion or acquired a new one, check your pulse, you may be dead."

~ Gelett Burgess

At what point do you decide you've had enough of living by rules that are contrary to a fulfilling, happy life? In the pursuit of transformation it will be necessary for you to challenge what you thought you knew. It was never intended for our thoughts, behaviors and beliefs to be a carbon copy of our parents or the generations before us. If we lived in a world where everyone just swallowed whole the beliefs and norms that came before us, evolution would have come to a screeching halt millions of years ago. The world would still be flat. Flight would still be impossible. Connecting with someone on the other side of the world through wireless electronic means would have you deemed delusional. Rules and the truth that held true and was appropriate for our parents' generation and their parents' generation don't necessarily hold true for us today. The only truth is constant change. We live in a world of constant change. We are constantly changing and evolving physically, spiritually and technologically. Past centered thinking, beliefs and practices will have you as Lot's wife was, immobilized and unable to move forward. The time is now for you to decide once and for all to rid yourself of the limiting parasitic labels and unauthentic roles that have contributed to your life of disconnect.

"The man who views the world at fifty the same as he did at twenty has wasted thirty years of life."

~ Muhammad Ali

Whenever I work with a client on challenging their belief system, I never take for granted that resisting the pull of the past can be the hardest struggle of a person's life. There always exists a sense of familiarity and comfort with the past regardless of how chaotic or dysfunctional it may have been. When you can make that shift from the comfort you find in familiarity to the excitement that exists in the possibility of the life that waits for you on the other side of transformation, you have made a giant leap for mankind!

As you commit to challenge what you know and reframe your belief system, consider the following scenarios as it relates to your parents or primary caregivers viewpoint on the world, happiness, work/career, personality, relationships/sex/marriage. Answer the questions corresponding to each category.

WORLDVIEW

Our parents' worldview, opinions and prejudices are shaped by the era and geographic location that they were born and raised. For example, parents born in the south during segregation are going to have a different worldview than parents born in a different era/geographic location. Just as parents who immigrated to the U.S. will tend to raise their children based on their country of origin's standards, norms and values. Your exploration is crucial to gaining a better understanding of what could have influenced your parents' beliefs, thus influencing yours.

I met Callie at the beginning of the second semester of my freshman year at Eastern Michigan University. Callie was a white female who lived in the honors dormitory with me. During a ceremony my dormitory had to commemorate the Martin Luther King, Jr. holiday, she bravely shared with the group that her parents had raised her to hate and fear minorities. College was the first experience and interaction that she had ever had with anyone outside of her racial group. Callie became emotional as she shared how her belief system over the first semester was not only shaken, but fell to pieces as she discovered many of the prejudice beliefs regarding minorities that she had were being challenged through the interactions and subsequent friendships she had formed.

1.   When and where were each of your parents born and raised? Be sure to include geographical location and any significant world or societal events that were occurring during this time. Did the era and location of their births influence any prejudices or beliefs they may have had?

HAPPINESS

People who experienced traumatic and unhappy childhoods don't miraculously become happy adults. A default mood of unhappiness is often carried on into adulthood and can infiltrate the quality of a person's parenting. If your parents grew up experiencing a difficult, unhappy childhood, their default setting and belief system is likely to be filled with unhappiness and pessimism which will undoubtedly be transferred to you.

2.   Did your mother have a happy childhood? Did your father? Describe both. Be sure to include any traumas or challenges either may have experienced such as poverty, discrimination, abuse, etc.

WORK/CAREER

Your parents' beliefs and attitudes about work helped to shape your beliefs. Was work regarded as simply a means to an end or were you encouraged to seek work that you found fulfilling? Were you expected to go into the family business or encouraged to spread your wings and find your passion? Growing up in inner city Detroit, it seemed that everyone's parents worked for one of the Big Three or some supplier of the industry. It was the norm for our parents to work 25-30 years in a factory setting that may not have been their passion but provided a good income. It was a common goal for many of my peers to transition into this industry after high school and many did, without considering if it would be work they were passionate about.

3.   **Where was each of your parents employed? Did they enjoy, tolerate, or hate it?**

PERSONALITY

Our personality type undoubtedly influences belief systems. For example, Mums are less comfortable with change. They tend to appreciate the structure and traditional norms than other personality types. Individuals who were raised by parents with a Mum personality type likely had significantly more rules and less flexibility growing up than individuals reared by other personality types. Now that you have a deeper appreciation of the different personality types, what personality type would you say your mother had? How about your father? Would you say your personality is similar or different than your parents?

4.   **Describe each parent's personality. Be as objective as possible.**

RELATIONSHIPS / SEX / MARRIAGE

Your viewpoints regarding marriage, intimacy and sex were influenced by what you were told, but even more so by what you observed. This is an area where many received contradictory messages between what may have been verbally communicated and what was actually witnessed.

Janelle was a 40 year-old woman whose frustration over yet another failed relationship had taken its toll on her. She wanted desperately to salvage her latest relationship that had been plagued with infidelity since the beginning. Surprisingly, my client did not regard the infidelity as the

problem in the relationship, but her partner's unwillingness to marry her. Janelle was so casual when she so matter-of-factly proclaimed in one of our sessions that every man cheats. My attempt to challenge this very damaging belief was met with a look by Janelle that suggested she pitied my naiveté. After exploring the origins of this belief, it was discovered that every woman in Janelle's life from her grandmother, mother, aunts and sisters all experienced continuous infidelity in their relationships. It was something in Janelle's words, that you "expect and deal with."

I have also encountered more examples than I can provide on the limiting beliefs regarding sex and intimacy. Women who can't escape the echo of their mother's or grandmother's voice regarding what "good girls" don't do has impacted their sexual expression with their partner. Or the echo of what may have been ingrained from religious institutions regarding women and sexuality resulting in countless individuals torn and riddled with guilt regarding their sexual preferences. Thomas was a 33 year-old male who initially came to see me with his fiancé. They had been engaged for six months and as his fiancé Cheryl expressed, their sex life, which had always been satisfying, had gone to the birds since the engagement. Thomas expressed that he truly loved and had always desired Cheryl sexually, but was now riddled with guilt over his sexual craving for her after he proposed. He explained how it was always impressed in him growing up that your wife is sacred and should not be regarded as a sexual object. Thomas expressed how he now saw his future wife as "*Madonna-like*." Unfortunately for Cheryl, he was not referencing the performer, but the religious figure. In response to the beliefs he had regarding appropriate sexuality a man is to have with his wife, Thomas could not bring himself to resume the fulfilling, electrically charged sexual relationship he once had with his fiancé. "After all," he stated, "Cheryl will one day be the mother of my children and the mother of my children wouldn't do the things that we used to do."

5.   **What would you guess as being your parent's attitudes about relationships?**

CHALLENGING FAULTY BELIEFS

In the timeless classic, *The Prophet*, philosopher Kahlil Gibran writes, "Your children are not your children...they come through you but not from you." He believed that parents are simply vessels for giving us life. Most of us were raised, however to believe just the opposite, that we are a direct extension of our parents, basically miniature carbon copies as children and mirror reflections of them as adults. Many find it difficult to separate their individual identity, beliefs and practices from the ones derived from our parents.

As stated earlier, there's no future in the past, which is why it is never advisable to dwell on it. There is however, understanding that can be gained by exploration. Many people are stuck in their past because there is a lack of understanding of why things happened the way they did. The exploration you just engaged in on the origins of your belief systems was intended to bring insight and understanding.

A fundamental error that exists in our society today is the fact that the majority of people who are struggling to empower themselves in this 21st century are still approaching life with a 20th century mentality that may have worked for their parents, but has become outdated, and downright detrimental to their own empowerment. Understanding the origins of your limiting beliefs gives you the courage to perform an honest appraisal of what beliefs are of value and which are of no value. After exploring with clients the origins of some of their, as well as their parents', limiting beliefs it becomes less threatening for them to challenge these beliefs. For some, questioning and challenging long-held family belief systems is regarded as the ultimate betrayal. It is imperative that you understand the intent is not to discount the invaluable lessons you received from your parents, but rather to examine the usefulness of those beliefs in your life currently. The hope is that you will discard the beliefs that are not adding value to your life while maintaining and creating beliefs that will be conducive to your life of fulfillment.

It is ultimately our belief about a situation, not the situation itself that influences our behavior. Our beliefs, whether empowering or limiting, determine our decisions. When discussing faulty thinking with my clients, I like to use the example of having someone driving too close behind you. We've all experienced someone driving so close behind your car that you fear they may rear-end you if you slow down. When I ask clients what their behavior is when this occurs they typically will respond with such statements as:

"I slow down."

"I give them a few choice words."

"I refuse to let them pass!"

When I question why they tend to choose this course of action, they respond with:

"Because that other driver was disrespecting me."

"Because the other driver wasn't respecting the rules of the road."

"Because that other driver was trying to control my driving and I'm not having it!"

I then ask what they would do if they discovered the driver behind them was rushing to the hospital because they had a child choking in the back seat. Immediately, their response to how they would respond in this situation changes to:

"I would move over and let them pass."

"I would call for help on my cell phone."

"If I could get them to stop, I would try to administer the Heimlich Maneuver."

When questioned as to why their behavior in that situation would change, unanimously they respond because they realize the person riding so close behind them is not being rude or disrespectful, but is a distraught parent trying to save the life of their child. I then ask them what about the situation has changed seeing that, the motorist is still driving too close behind them. The fact that they no longer believe the other driver was disrespecting or attempting to control them has led to the modification of their behavior. It is this realization that brings home the fact that it is ultimately your belief about a situation that influences your behavior, not the situation itself.

Initial Reaction:

Situation	Belief	Response/Behavior
Motorist riding your bumper	You are being disrespected Person is rude	Slow down Don't allow them to pass Curse

After challenging your belief system:

Situation	Belief	Response/Behavior
Motorist riding your bumper	The motorist is a concerned parent The motorist is rightfully frightened and in a hurry	You move over to let the motorist pass You call 911 on your cell phone You try to be of help

Changing our beliefs about any situation changes our response to that situation. Of course, most of us will have no way of knowing what the motivation is behind a motorist who is driving too close behind us. If it is however your automatic tendency to embrace a belief that results in defensive, combative behavior, you may want to question what other areas of your life are you allowing your behavior to be negatively impacted by your faulty beliefs.

Research supports that one of the most effective ways of treating depression and anxiety is to challenge individuals limiting, pessimistic, defeating beliefs and thoughts. Depression and anxiety are maintained by our beliefs and thoughts. Depressed individuals will often times unconsciously seek out events and situations that maintain their belief that life is hopeless. Individuals struggling with depression watch the news far more than non-depressed individuals. For some, it becomes compulsive. They watch the morning news, the five o'clock news, the six o'clock news then switch over to a news network before turning back to the eleven o'clock news before bedtime. They give great attention to the tragic stories regarding increased crime, innocent by-standers being victimized, global warming, failing economy, etc. Any story that supports their belief that life is sad and hopeless is given attention. These stories reinforce what they already believe, that they indeed have a reason and right to be depressed. Some may take it a step further and call family members and friends to share the endless stories of mayhem and despair they watched on the news.

Situation	Belief	Response/Behavior
Watching hours upon hours of news	The world is a bad place Life is hopeless We have no control over what happens to us	Remain depressed Give up No motivation Share with others your depressed outlook

You hold on to limiting beliefs for one of two reasons. Either those beliefs were so ingrained in you that deviation from it would be like cutting off a limb, or your personal experiences have reinforced these limiting beliefs over time. Crucial to challenging limiting beliefs involves understanding the origins of your beliefs and reconfiguring the beliefs that are not conducive to your growth and well-being.

Our beliefs can be passed down like genes. They become a genetic blueprint. Consider the following scenarios of two families. Family #1 appears to be able to remain optimistic through some of the most challenging circumstances, appearing to always come out on top, recovering from life's difficulties. Family #2 appears to be the poster child for misfortune, a target for repeated tragedies that they can't quite recover from before the next tragedy strikes. Instead of picking up the pieces and progressing in life as Family #1 does, Family #2 remains stuck, never seeming to get ahead. The next generation of Family #2 doesn't fare much better than the generation before them. Life is a constant stream of misfortune with few and short-lived breaks in between.

I've had clients explain their misfortunes in life by professing with absolute certainty that they come from a cursed family. I've even heard the concept "generational curses" being used in religious settings, which doesn't do much to alleviate a person's hopeless and helpless disposition. What they fail to realize is this "curse" they speak of is nothing more than their limiting beliefs and thoughts that prevents them from experiencing a more fulfilling outcome. Whatever is happening to you at any given moment is a by-product of your beliefs and thoughts.

The end of dwelling in your past and adhering to faulty beliefs and thoughts is here. Now that you have understanding, you can let the past go. There is no need to re-work it or poke around in it. You can shed the skin of your past because you are now aware that it serves no purpose. Your waking hours were never intended to be bogged down by chronic thinking or faulty beliefs. As stated earlier in this chapter, your existence was intended to be one of conscious awareness. Now that you recognize the risks that exists with living unconsciously through faulty thinking and limiting beliefs, you can begin to take the necessary action to living a more consciously aware life. In the next chapter, Step #3: Making Sense of Your Senses, you will be introduced to techniques that will lead to a more conscious, thus more rewarding life.

CHAPTER THREE

STEP 3: MAKING SENSE OF YOUR SENSES

"All credibility, all good conscience, all evidence of truth come only from the senses."

~ Friedrich Nietzsche

As discussed in Step 2, living life in a consciously aware state was intended to be our natural state of being. Even if you've never considered this before, at some deep, ethereal level, your body, mind and spirit knows this. Despite the constant thinking we engage in, unconsciously we are in constant pursuit of returning to our intended state of conscious awareness. It is through conscious awareness that we are able to shut down all the mind chatter. Constant thinking, as discussed, produces pain, anxiety, despair, depression and *dis*-ease. Conscious awareness elicits calmness, contentment, joy and exhilaration. Our bodies know this and despite the reckless tendency to forego this natural state of being, there is an ever-present longing to experience peaks of conscious awareness through all our unconscious living.

In an attempt to self-correct and produce moments of conscious awareness in our lives, many people stumble upon destructive behaviors that elicit feelings of being in the now. Some of the most prevalent behaviors that exist in our society today that produces moments of conscious awareness include drug abuse, gambling, overeating, pathological shopping, and hoarding. All of these behaviors and many more that are too extensive to list at this time have become so problematic in our society because of the artificial connection to conscious awareness it provides.

While completing my doctoral internship, I had the invaluable experience of counseling women who were part of a residential drug treatment program. Many of the women, who were on their second, third, fourth and even fifth attempt at sobriety, expressed their genuine desire to end their addiction. Most of the women in the program had experienced a lifetime of traumatic events that began in childhood and only multiplied once their addiction began. Repeatedly, the women would express how the drugs worked so well at shutting their minds down. The memories of their traumatic events and constant thinking of the past and how disappointing their lives had become did not occur when they were high on the drugs. They would express how the high allowed them to just be— no stress, no depression, no anxiety—just be. This sense of being or conscious awareness would last only as long as the high lasted and then all the pain of their past and disappointment of their present would come flooding back in even stronger than before, leading them to seek out the high yet again. I can distinctly remember one woman telling me almost as if she had an epiphany while leaving our session, that when she actively engaged in smoking, injecting or snorting her drug, she would experience a connection to God. Her ability to live in the moment and experience the connected feeling that accompanies conscious awareness was now contingent upon her addiction.

In a society where obesity has become an epidemic, scientists, psychologists and medical professionals are scurrying to uncover the causes. Less exercises, unhealthy food choices, and larger food portions have all been thrown around as tangible culprits. However, the emotional connection that exists with food is often the least discussed factor. Any person who finds themself significantly overweight has developed an unhealthy connection to food. They are not eating because they are hungry. They are eating because the process of eating connects them to conscious awareness. When engaging in the process of eating, their mind is able to be in the moment. Their senses are tuned in. They find themselves relishing the tastes, texture and smell of the food. Their mind is not on the past or present in that active moment of eating. They are able to experience a peak of conscious awareness while eating just as the person who is in an inebriated stupor caused by some drug feels a sense of just being. The same is true of countless other behaviors that have now become problematic in our society because of the connection between that behavior and the ability to achieve a return to the natural state of conscious awareness.

USING YOUR FIVE SENSES TO ACHIEVE CONSCIOUS AWARENESS

One of the most effective ways to achieve and maintain conscious awareness is to regularly connect with your senses: sight, sound, touch, taste and smell. These five senses begin communicating to us well before we make our grand entrance into the world. The data we receive from our senses are crucial in our ability to learn, navigate, and respond to cues that will ensure our survival. As we grow older, many of us take for granted the fact that our five senses are tools that help us better function in life to not only increase our chances of survival, but to allow for a more pleasurable existence. Each of our senses function independently and interdependently to help protect us from harm, help us navigate our environment and allow for conscious awareness.

"I do not feel obliged to believe that the same God who has endowed us with sense, reason, and intellect has intended us to forgo their use."

~ Galileo Galilee

The value of the five senses in our daily lives is evident in everyday living. From the time we awaken, our five senses are operating to assist us in every daily activity we engage in, from the routine procedure of brushing our teeth to the more complex process of maneuvering through rush hour traffic. Consider the following scenario: If while reading this book, you begin to smell smoke, you would most likely put this book down and go investigate where the smoke was coming from. If, while investigating, you saw flames coming from your neighbor's home, you would likely call the fire department. While waiting for the fire department to arrive, you run to your neighbor's door. Upon touching the doorknob you nearly burn your hand due to the temperature of the doorknob. This communicates to you that the heat inside is much too hot for you to attempt to enter. Panicked, you begin to fear the worst. Then you hear someone call your name. As you turn, you see it is your neighbor who has made it out of their home safely. The four senses utilized: smell, sight, touch and sound were instrumental in helping to avert danger.

Our senses are consistently communicating to us, assisting us as we navigate our world. Hearing a bump in the night, will prompt us to awaken, as would a crying baby or the sunlight peaking through our window. Tasting food that is too hot for us, prompts us to wait until it cools down as would tasting milk that has soured would prompt us to discard of it. The fact that our senses are invaluable tools that help us function and survive in this complex world becomes apparent early on in our lives. Despite there being people who have learned quite successfully to navigate their life on a daily basis without the use of one or sometimes more of their senses, most of us shudder at the thought of life with an absent sense. We know there are accommodations that could be implemented. Individuals who have lost their sense of sight learn to use Braille and deaf individuals learn sign language to connect with their environment. Accommodations such as Braille and sign language and to a lesser severity, eyeglasses, came about because of the necessity to have our five senses functioning at their most optimal level.

In recent years, medical technology has given some individuals who have spent a lifetime blind or deaf the ability for the first time in their lives to see and hear. Many of these miraculous moments have been video recorded and shared with the world. Watching a person see visual images or hear sound for the first time in their life is an overwhelming moment, to say the least. After having some time to adapt to their environment with their newfound senses, individuals will always invariably mention the phenomenon of having their world, and the possibilities that exist in it, open up exponentially as a result.

CONNECTING TO CONSCIOUS AWARENESS

An exercise you can engage in to promote conscious awareness is to spend a few minutes everyday deliberately connecting to your five senses. You choose what time of day and in what environment. You can engage in this exercise anytime of the day as an exercise to increase moments of conscious awareness. It is also a good idea to engage in this exercise whenever you notice your thoughts have become consumed with thinking that is purposeless and non-productive.

Begin by selecting one of your five senses to focus upon. Let's use the sense of sight as an example. Look around you. What do you see? Focus on every aspect of the visual images that are being communicated to you by your environment. If you are outside, look at the trees, notice their movement in the wind. Notice the color of your neighbor's front door or the contours of the car that just drove by. It may be the form of your own hand that you visually examine, the length of each finger or perhaps you choose to turn your hand over and examine the lines in your palm. Now move on to the next sense, let's say sound. What do you hear? If you are at home, perhaps it is the sound of your dog breathing or the hum of the clothes dryer with the occasional sound of a metal zipper hitting the steel drum inside. Is it the sound of a plane flying above? Move on to the sense of smell. Are there any particular scents that fill the room? Perhaps the aroma of last night's dinner or the bouquet of flowers that sits on your bedside table lingers. What about touch? What do you feel against your skin? Is it the coolness of your bed sheets or the irritation of your wool coat? You may decide to touch the surface of a nearby object and notice the feel. Is it cool, warm, smooth or jagged? What about the temperature around you? Are you warm, cold or content? Scan your body. Is there pain in any particular area or are there parts of your body that feel especially relaxed? Lastly, scan your sense of taste. Is there any taste that lingers on your taste buds such as the mint flavor of your toothpaste? Perhaps you want to grab a piece of fruit or take a sip of your morning tea and really tune into the flavors as they connect with your taste buds. The intent is to connect to your environment utilizing each of your five senses. Notice how your mind quiets as you attend to what is now and present in the moment. As you connect to your environment, you become consciously aware.

The goal is to begin consciously attending to your world by engaging in this exercise throughout the day. There are times you will tune to one sense more than the other, and that is perfectly fine. As I take walks through my neighborhood, I will tune into the four senses of sight, sound, smell and touch. I visually tune into the trees that line the streets, colors of the flowers and shrubs that border homes. I give attention to any unique yard designs or ornaments. I listen to the barking of dogs, the laughter of children playing, the birds chirping. I relish in the smell of apple blossoms in the springtime or fresh baked cookies that emanate from the local bakery. I pay attention to the feel of the sun against my face, or the cool breeze the wind provides. If it happens to rain, I feel the raindrops as they fall against my skin. A thirty-minute walk provides me with a steady flow of conscious awareness through the utilization of my senses.

As you increase these moments of connecting with conscious awareness you will find you are more able to live in the moment and your pathological thinking will decrease. Remember the goal is not to eliminate all thought. That would be foolish and detrimental in it's own right. Thought that involves planning and strategy is crucial to our evolution, growth and survival. It was engaging in thought that spearheaded the Wright brothers strategically creating the first airplane and Edison inventing the first light bulb. It is thought that goes behind your planning to relocate to another state, seek out new employment or navigate to the other side of town. Thought is crucial and necessary, but only for the intent of strategy or planning. As indicated in Chapter Two, thought should only be a small portion of our conscious daily living. Thought has never been considered one of our five senses because the intent of thought is not to operate continuously as our five senses do. We were intended to control our thoughts, not the other way around.

Following is a list of activities you can engage to connect to your senses and achieve conscious awareness:

SIGHT
Watching the sunrise/sunset
Watching flames in a fireplace
Watching the stars in the sky
Watching the waves in the ocean
Relishing in the brilliance of Fall colors
Watching falling snowflakes
Watching clouds moving in the sky

SOUND
Listening to water (waterfall, ocean waves, babbling brook, rain)
Rustling of leaves
Blowing wind
Soothing music
Sound of crickets on a summer night
Children's laughter

TOUCH
Making love Feeling the sand between your toes Feeling the sun warm your body Warm bubble bath Cool pillow on a hot summer night Relaxing massage

TASTE
Fresh fruit Herbal tea Fine wine Fresh squeezed orange juice Fresh baked cookies

SMELL
Fresh flowers Summer rain Spring blossoms Ocean air Scented candles Fresh cut grass

THE SIXTH SENSE

What if I told you that you have been navigating this world unaware of another sense that is just as crucial to your survival and success as your other five senses? What if you discovered that like those fortunate individuals who are able to see and hear for the first time in their lives, you could access this new sense? What if I told you that this new sense would make life easier to navigate? You would make less wrong turns and avoid many of the frustrating dead-ends and crises you find yourself in. Whereas most of us would be devastated at the thought of navigating this world without one of our five senses, we fail to realize that most of us have done just that in living a life without utilizing our sixth sense of intuition.

Intuition is inherent in all creatures from salmon who can find their way hundreds and even thousands of miles back to their original spawning place, to birds who instinctively know when to fly south. The basic caterpillar is intuitively aware when the time has come to build the cocoon around itself and transform into a butterfly. Studies have long recorded the tendency many animals have to be aware of events before they happen. This foresight is evident in your basic pet dog who will go sit at the door precisely as its owner is returning home apparently having some awareness of the owner's arrival that extends beyond its five senses. Animals spontaneously by the masses leaving locations, has long been a foreboding warning of potential disaster, such as an earthquake, volcanic activity and tsunami. It has often been documented that not only pets, but, wild animals such as monkeys and elephants will instinctively leave an area prior to a natural disaster taking place. A 2005 *National Geographic* article documented eyewitness accounts of animal behavior before the devastating tsunami that originated in the Indian Ocean. According to eyewitnesses in the days leading up to the tsunami, elephants screamed and ran for higher ground, dogs refused to go outside and zoo animals rushed into their shelters and could not be enticed to come back out. In one particular wildlife reserve which was home to leopards, elephants and 130 species of birds, scientists did not see any animal remains with the exception of two water buffalos that had died. More than 150,000 people were killed in this December 2004 natural disaster, however, relatively few animals were reported dead.

Animals are so "in tune" with the earth that they can sense and avoid potentially devastating situations. As humans, we possess the potential to utilize our intuition to not only avoid potentially devastating situations, but to thrive and become successful. In the course of human evolution we unfortunately got out of tune with our intuition. This sixth sense of intuition was pushed from our awareness by an overreliance on thinking. As we evolved into modern day society with all of its logic and analysis, intuition wasn't included in the textbooks or discussed in families. This has been more of a catastrophic disservice to us than most realize. Again, imagine if someone had blindfolded your eyes at birth and you had no knowledge of this thing called sight until the blindfold was removed many years later. Imagine how much your world would have changed instantaneously. You would have capabilities and advantages that never before existed for you. This is what happens when you decide to take the reigns off your intuition. A world with entirely new possibilities opens up.

Intuition can best be described as the immediate insight you receive about yourself, another person, a situation or your environment. It's that gut feeling that can't be explained, but is real nevertheless. Often times, when treating my clients, I will have an immediate stroke of intuitive insight about their situation that seems to come out of the blue. This intuition will typically send the focus of the session in an entirely different direction that is precisely the direction needed to maximize my client's insight thus accelerating the accomplishment of their goals. We've all experienced our intuition at work, however, unlike the five senses, intuition is all too often dismissed as irrelevant because we can't precisely pinpoint it. We will talk ourselves out of validating our intuitive feeling failing to realize that listening and responding accordingly to our intuition can be a life-saver.

MOTHER'S INTUITION

It was 4:00 in the morning when I was awakened by a voice. It was not audible in the way we normally hear. It was more of an internal voice telling me to get up and of all things, take a pregnancy test. I remember laughing to myself as I turned over and went back to sleep, thinking to myself that I must have been dreaming. Forty minutes later, once again the voice awakened me from my sleep.

"Get up and take a pregnancy test." Once again, I dismissed this voice, not really knowing how to explain it, but knowing that there was no way I was getting out of my comfortable bed to follow the commands of something so silly, especially when I still had at least another three good hours of sleep to get in. At five thirty that morning the relentless voice returned, only this time it was more urgent, *"GET UP AND TAKE A PREGNANCY TEST!"* I sat up in my bed and looked around, not frightened, but embarrassed at the weirdness of it all. I had no reason to believe I was pregnant. I was not even late for my period, but it was apparent that whatever this thing was it was not going to leave me alone. I remember thinking to myself, "I'd better get out of this bed and take a pregnancy test if I want to get any sleep."

With my eyes half-closed, I went to my hallway closet, fumbled around and found a pregnancy test that had been a gag-gift at a party I had attended about a year earlier. After struggling to get the stick out of the foil wrapper and following the instructions in my half-sleep state, I waited the three minutes to see the results. One dark pink line appeared and that was it, no second line. I felt so foolish to have actually gotten out of my bed and followed such a ridiculous command. I shook my head and laughed as I threw the test away and went back to bed.

I hadn't been sleep for thirty minutes when, you guessed it, the voice returned. *"Go get the test out of the garbage!"* it commanded.

"You've gotta be kidding me," I thought. I was getting irritated at this point. As if it wasn't bad enough that I had some unexplainable voice telling me what to do, but it seemed to be taking some type of pleasure in interrupting my sleep to make a fool out of me. I pulled the comforter over my head hoping to silence the voice, but as I mentioned, it was not a voice coming from the outside. It was more internal. As much as I wanted to ignore whatever this was, I was bewildered by this unexplainable experience. I knew if nothing else, this inner-voice was persistent and was not going to be satisfied until I did as it said.

In a surrendered attitude I once again got out of the bed, went to my bathroom, reached in the garbage and retrieved the stick. To my astonishment, two dark pink lines were showing in the window. I looked at the test in disbelief. Unable to go back to sleep, I anxiously waited for the local drug store to open. I bought two more tests which both read positive as well. I had no idea of what to make of this situation until I remembered that just one day prior I had gone to my doctor complaining of ear and throat pain. He had diagnosed me with a sinus infection and prescribed a powerful course of antibiotics that if had been taken while pregnant would have potentially caused serious birth defects. It then became apparent that the inner-voice was indeed my intuition protecting both me, and my son from potentially devastating consequences.

We've all heard stories of intuition at work. Someone deciding for no apparent reason to take a different route to work only to discover later that the bridge they typically cross daily in their regular route collapsed at precisely the time they would have been crossing it. A study of train crashes over a five-year period showed that on the days when there were accidents, the number of passengers on the train was significantly less than usual. In one case, the average was 65 passengers, and on the day of the crash there were only nine passengers on board. There were a lot of people avoiding those trains without any explanation.

The doomed Titanic sailed with only 58 percent of her total capacity of passengers. Many people cancelled their reservations in the weeks prior to the sailing. There are countless stories of individuals who worked in the Twin Towers oversleeping or missing their train or just deciding not to go into the office on September 11, 2001. A 2008 *Science Daily* article entitled, "Go With Your Gut – Intuition is More Than Just a Hunch" discussed this phenomenon, which is not such a phenomenon considering intuition has been a part of the human experience since the beginning of man. This article discusses how we all experience a 'gut feeling' that we can't explain or shake. The experience of instantly loving or hating a new house, new job or new person we meet. Researchers at Leeds say these hunches, or intuitions are real and should be taken seriously. According to the article, "*In recent years, the subject of intuition has emerged from obscurity.*

Intuition is increasingly recognized as a natural mental faculty, a key element in the creative process, a means of discovery, problem solving, and decision-making. Once considered the province of a gifted few, it is now recognized as an innate capacity available to everyone not a rare, accidental talent, but a natural skill anyone can cultivate."

Anything beyond the five senses can be difficult for people to accept. Many will subscribe to the attitude of "If I can't hear it, see it, touch it, taste it or smell it, then it doesn't exist." Truth is you can't see molecules or atoms, but you know that they exist. I've never met a person who has seen God, but billions of people on the planet believe in a higher power. We believe in the existence of many things we can't see or measure, but through our experience we know they exist. The acknowledgment of the existence of your intuition is the first step in accessing its benefit. Intuition connects you to conscious awareness. It allows you to plug into the knowledge of the universe. There is no limits to what a person who learns to master their intuition can achieve.

In her lecture, *From Intellect to Intuition*, Jane Hart likens unleashing and cultivating your intuition to discovering you have another arm you never knew you had. She challenges lecture participants to imagine unknowingly, going through life with one arm tied behind your back until someone says, "Hey, you have another arm back here!" and unties it. You would be amazed and grateful at how much more you can do with two hands and two arms than you were able to do with one.

INTUITION IN DISCOVERY

The connection between intellect and intuition is one of the greatest wonders of the universe. It is intuition that has spearheaded our evolution. Some of the greatest discoveries, innovations and masterpieces known to mankind are credited to have occurred during intuitive insight. Countless inventors, scientists and artists who struggled to find the solutions to their craft similarly report how answers and insights seemed to come out of nowhere, often times long after they had shut their intellectual mind down. Isaac Newton reportedly watched an apple fall from a tree and made a connection between the motion of the apple and the gravitational pull between the moon and earth. Penicillin was discovered as a result of a contamination accident in a Petri dish containing bacteria. The discovery of this led to the first true miracle drug. If it had not been for many of these flashes of intuitive insights we would still be in the Stone Age.

Einstein is quoted as saying, "The only real valuable thing is intuition." He considered the intuitive mind a sacred gift and the rational mind a faithful servant. According to Einstein, "We have created a society that honors the servant and has forgotten the gift." Tuning into your intuition provides you with more capability than you can imagine. Intuition provides you with a vantage point. It's like being at the top of a watchtower that overlooks the landscape of your life. When you stand at the top of this watchtower you have a clear view of every direction. You can see what's coming ahead as well as what's approaching from behind. As you observe the ins and outs of your life, intuitively from this watchtower, you become more aware of potential pitfalls and are able to avoid catastrophic situations you may have unknowingly walked directly into if you did not have this vantage point. Intuition positions you to receive a steady stream of valuable information. We are all hard-wired to receive information through our intuitive sense. However, just because we are hard-wired to receive it doesn't mean we will. Just as you can have a home hard-wired with an intercom system, if you choose never to turn that system on, you will never experience the benefit of it. Intuition must be acknowledged, activated and accessed. Living life in tune with your intuition equips you to make better decisions, greater discoveries and solve problems more creatively. Embracing intuition will support your personal transformation and move you toward your goals with a lot less effort and a lot more accuracy than you've become accustomed to.

One important aspect to keep in mind when learning to incorporate intuition into your life is that your intuition will sometimes guide you to do things and move in directions that you may not want to move in. The very thing that you may have tried to avoid and ignore for so long may very well be the very thing you must do to ensure a more successful outcome for yourself. It may be your intuition encouraging you to leave a comfortable, familiar relationship. You may talk yourself out of enduring the pain and hurt that invariably comes with a break-up. You may question the practical value of stepping away from something that you've attached yourself to, but it may very well be this relationship that prevents your successful transformation. When your intuition is guiding you to do something that may initially cause more pain than pleasure, such as leaving a relationship, job, geographic location, etc. it is imperative to return to that watchtower and take a glimpse of the life that awaits you once you've navigated through the pain.

UNCOVERING YOUR INTUITIVE STYLE

We have all received intuitive messages at some time in our lives. Intuition may come in many forms. People experience intuition in three ways: visually, verbally or feeling. They visually see images in their dreams or in images in their environment that spark some intuitive insight. They may hear that inner or "little voice" which guides them in the most beneficial direction. Individuals will discuss the 'gut-feeling' that prompts them to act. For some, intuition is accompanied by goose bumps or the hair standing up on their arms or the back of their necks to indicate they've just experienced a deeper knowing that can't be explained.

Visual intuition can occur in your waking hours, as it did with Isaac Newton's intuitive insight on gravity. Individuals can see something in their environment that would ordinarily be considered relatively benign but sparks some innovation, discovery or important information. Artists, scientists, decorators, designers can relate to having their inspiration coming from the most unexpected stimulus. Visual intuition can also occur during the dream state. Some dreams are simply your intuition communicating to you at a time when you are more apt to receive the information, in the still of the night, in your dream state. Intuition in the dream state can provide direction, warning and guidance.

In my late twenties, I interviewed for a promotion in the government agency I worked for. It wasn't necessarily a position that I desired, but it came with an increased salary. Despite other candidates having decades more experience than me, I got the position. I had colleagues all over the state telling me how proud they were for me being the youngest person in the history of the agency to hold the position. Within the first few days of my new role, I began having second thoughts. Despite the position coming with an increased salary and the potential for even further advancement in the agency, it just didn't feel right. It was a job not well suited for my personality and not in alignment with the direction I wanted my career to go in. However, there was no way I was going to walk away from it. The combination of the honor that came with being chosen for the position and the commitment I made to accept it resigned me to just grin and bear it. About a month into the position, I went to sleep and had a very vivid dream of my late grandmother Rosie. She was sitting at a table enjoying a meal. She looked very content and had a smile on her face. She then looked up from her meal directly at me smiling a wide grin and shaking her head "No." There was not one word uttered in the dream yet, intuitively, I knew my grandmother was telling me to resign from the job and reassuring me that everything would be fine. The next morning, just after awakening, I contacted my supervisor and told him that I was resigning. Surprisingly, there was no apprehension in my decision. I was able to resume my former position and within a year, I started a position in a completely different agency that was more fitting with my career goals. Some years later, grandma Rosie visited me again. Pregnant with my third child and with two boys already, I desperately wanted a girl. She appeared in my dream holding a baby in her arms, once again, not saying a word, she simply held the baby up and revealed a baby wearing a pink hat. Two months later, it was revealed in an ultrasound that I was indeed having a girl.

The most vivid experience of an intuitive knowing that I've experienced occurred in the summer of 2002. For several weeks, leading into August 2002 I had an uneasy feeling of sadness. I remember sharing this unsettling feeling with a few of my friends, one of which suggested I fast from dusk to dawn to encourage clarity. I had never fasted for clarity before but the strong feeling of despair I was experiencing was unlike anything I had felt before and I was willing to try anything to bring an end to that uncomfortable feeling. During the course of this week long dusk to dawn fast, my dad was admitted to the hospital for pneumonia which was not an uncommon affliction for him being that he had spent so many years immobilized by his stroke. Within a couple of days, his condition improved and he was scheduled to be discharged from the hospital. The evening before his discharge, he was more coherent and lucid than I had seen him in a while. I visited him with my mother and watched him finish off his dinner while totally engrossed in watching the movie *Life* with Eddie Murphy that was playing on his hospital television. I can remember him adamantly gesturing to me to move out of the way when I stepped in front of the television monitor. It was always nice to see him in the peaks of lucidity he would occasionally experience. Before leaving his hospital room, I blew him a kiss. He diverted his attention from the movie that had him so engaged, extended his right arm up to catch my kiss and placed it on his heart.

Later that evening, after returning from the hospital, that gnawing feeling of despair and sadness I had been experiencing for the past week or so became even stronger. In fact, it was so strong that I began unexpectedly crying while sitting on my patio. I just could not seem to get it together that evening. The next morning I called into the office and cancelled all my appointments for that day. This was totally out of the ordinary for me. I rarely missed work, but something was telling me that I needed to do it.

My father was scheduled for discharge later on that afternoon, but something compelled me to go to the hospital that morning. When I made it to my father's room, the nurse informed me that he had just been taken down for a scheduled endoscopy and he should be back within a half-hour. I headed back to the waiting area on the main floor. As I stepped off the elevator I was hit with a feeling that nearly knocked me off my feet. I remember immediately and without deliberate thought saying, "God, let thy will be done." All of a sudden the cloud of despair that had plagued me seemed to lift.

As I sat, waiting for the nurse to page me upon my dad's return, thirty minutes became an hour, an hour became an hour and a half. While skimming through magazines to pass time, a voice communicated to me that my fast was over and that I should go get one of those fresh baked brownies that was smelling so good in the hospital's coffee shop. I chuckled to myself. Just then, I received a page from the nurses' station instructing me to go to the waiting area on my father's floor. In this waiting room sat two doctors, a nurse and a chaplain who informed me something had gone terribly wrong and my father had died during the procedure.

As the weeks went by and I started connecting the dots of the events leading up to his death, there was no doubt in my mind that it was intuition, my gut feeling, that was both warning and preparing me for my father's death. I know it was my intuition that guided me to not only take the day off from work, but to go to the hospital at the time I did. As devastating as his unexpected death was, there is a sense of comfort to know that I was present in the hospital when he made his transition. Knowing the sense of humor my dad always had, I am convinced that it was him telling me to go grab that delicious brownie.

As you reflect on your own intuitive experiences, what would you say your intuitive style is? Is your intuition communicated visually, or by the little voice or gut feeling?

INTUITION, INSTINCT, or PREMONITION

It is not uncommon for clients and seminar participants to question the difference between intuition and the even more controversial phenomenon of premonition. For some, the examples I've shared of intuition at play in my life may seem more of an example of premonition than intuition. From the inner-voice urging me to take a pregnancy test, my late grandmother showing up in my dreams to give me information and guidance, to the apparent forewarning I had prior to my father's death. What qualifies these examples as intuition and what separates them from instinct or premonition? A working definition of intuition is insight, understanding or knowing about something without engaging in thought to arrive at that insight, understanding or knowing. Premonition is best defined as an advance warning or feeling that something is going to happen. Instinct is defined as an intuitive way of responding. One could argue that the examples used are more indicative of intuition while others feel premonition is more at play. The risk in such a debate is that it overshadows the inherent gift of all these phenomena that falls under the sixth sense. Intuition, premonition and instinct are all products of our sixth sense, a connection to something greater than our five physical senses are able to perceive. It matters less which phenomenon is operating and more that you acknowledge and access this wondrous gift that will give you an invaluable advantage in your life.

WAYS TO STRENGTHEN YOUR SIXTH-SENSE

One way to strengthen and better access your sixth sense ability is by engaging in activities that connect and enhance your other five senses. This consequently makes your sixth sense stronger. Following are some practical suggestions:

Practice Conscious awareness. As discussed in Chapter Two, living in the moment connects you to your immediate environment. When you are consciously aware you are better able to receive the signals from all of your senses, including the sixth sense.

Be open-minded and non-judgmental. Unfortunately, the concept of the sixth sense has received a bad rap due to misconceptions that were perpetuated throughout history by society and some religious institutions. These misconceptions and myths have led to many being very resistant to the idea of sixth-sense phenomenon. Resistance is one surefire way to stifle your intuition, premonition and instinctual knowing. Challenging limiting beliefs and being open-minded is crucial for strengthening this sense.

Unleash the kid in you. Engaging in artistic activities like coloring, doodling, singing and just old fashion play activates the right side of your brain which is believed to be the part of the brain activated when we are utilizing our sixth sense. Our society has become so left-brain dominant with all our logical and concrete thinking that our right brain has suffered atrophy. Just as a muscle that isn't utilized becomes weak, our right brain is not being engaged enough. Revert back to childhood activities like playing a game of jacks, drawing or staring at the sky watching the clouds form in and out of shape. This is a sure fire way to build that right brain muscle thus strengthening your sixth sense.

Write it down. Write down ideas, words or phrases that come to you when you are brainstorming or problem solving. Brainstorming and problem solving involves thinking and it is this function that thought is intended for. However, it is not uncommon to have flashes of intuition or premonition sandwiched between our thoughts. Writing down whatever comes to mind gives you an opportunity to recognize this when it occurs. Often times insight and information from the sixth sense will come so spontaneously, even when you are not brainstorming or problem solving, that it can be easily forgotten.

Practice guessing. A game I like to play with my daughters when we are near elevators is to guess what elevator will be the first to arrive, or what will be the color of the next car that passes us or who will be the next person that calls the home phone. These are all fun exercises that builds your sixth sense. Over time you will be amazed at how accurate your guesses begin to become.

Observe others. As you encounter others, be it in the workplace, at home or in public places like restaurants or stores, notice their non-verbal behaviors, facial expressions and gestures. As you observe, try to tune into the person. What are they feeling? What might they be thinking? What is the first feeling that comes to your mind regarding this person? Are they happy, sad, excited or hurried. With clients, family and friends I use my intuition to gather information regarding what they may be experiencing at any given moment. Cultivating your sixth sense is not just beneficial for you. Over time, you will learn that your sixth sense ability will be a tool that benefits others as much as it benefits you. You will get messages, guidance or gut-feelings about others that they may not be able to access due to their resistance or blocked emotional state.

Meditate. Meditation is the surest, quickest way to connect to your sixth sense. The importance of meditation cannot be underestimated. In her bestselling book, *Eat, Pray, Love*, author Elizabeth Gilbert asserts that prayer is the act of speaking to God and meditation is the act of listening. You are more able to tune into the frequency of your sixth sense when you meditate regularly. Chapter Six will discuss meditation in more detail.

EMOTIONAL POSITIONING SYSTEM

Recognizing and honoring your emotions, even the ones you may consider the "bad" emotions is a great way to tune your intuition. One of the biggest errors in modern day education is the lack of attention that is given to emotional intelligence. We are taught the three R's of arithmetic, reading and writing. Our intelligence quotient or IQ has traditionally been based on our ability to assimilate, apply and navigate these fundamentals. It has been a long-held belief that it is an individual's IQ that best determines his success in life. In Daniel Goleman's 1995 best-selling book, *Emotional Intelligence*, he proposed that a person's success in life is more determined by their emotional intelligence than their academic intelligence. This point is brought home when we hear the tragic story of some ivy-league scholar who takes his or her life after receiving a "B" in a class. This event leaves so many wrought with confusion wondering how such a smart person could make such an unwise decision. There is a lack of understanding because many are unable to separate academic intelligence from emotional intelligence. Whereas this student may have excelled academically, he or she lacked the necessary ingredients of emotional intelligence, which has more bearing on their success in life than their grades.

For most of us, the only thing we were ever taught about emotions either formally or informally, is that good emotions were good and didn't tend to cause problems and that bad emotions were bad and should be avoided at all costs. We were never told that our ability to manage our emotions has a direct bearing on our success in life. Our success in our career, relationships, health and wealth is contingent on our ability to manage and be guided by our emotions. Emotions are not intended to be suppressed, but acknowledged so they can guide your next move. Unfortunately, many engage in suppressing their emotions through illegal drugs, alcohol, and prescription medications including psychotropic medications. The suppression of your emotions keeps you stuck, in a state of limbo. When you suppress your emotions you unable to be guided in the next best direction for you. It's no surprise that the increasing number of people struggling with addiction correlates with the economic collapse, collapse of the family, collapse of the educational system and the health crisis. Solutions can't be achieved in a state of limbo. As people become less and less able to manage their emotions effectively, we will continue to struggle to be successful as a nation and a world.

What, if anything, were you taught about your emotions? Many men were raised and reinforced throughout their lives to suppress emotions such as sadness, which is why sadness for men is often times expressed as anger, a more socially acceptable emotion for them. Women, on the other hand, were taught that sadness was not only an acceptable emotion for them, but should be talked about, which is why so many more women seek therapy than men. To some degree or another, we were all taught which emotions were acceptable to feel and which were not. This approach is flawed because all emotions are valuable, from anger to joy, because they provide us with invaluable information that can be utilized to navigate and be successful in life.

The second aspect of making sense of your senses is learning to utilize your emotions as you would utilize a map or in more modern day, a GPS or Global Positioning System to get you to your desired location. Our emotions are a primitive, yet very sophisticated navigation system that is always operating to guide us. Our emotions communicate to us if we should proceed with something or turn in an entirely new direction. Both good and bad emotions are data, and like the data we receive from our GPS system, our EPS or Emotional Positioning System guides us in the best direction to go in. Feelings like happiness, bliss, joy, enthusiasm, and confidence are our EPS communicating to us that we are in a good position and to proceed with whatever it is that is eliciting the good feelings. It's as if a universal satellite is communicating back to you to that you are on the right track, keep going, don't veer off the lane you are in. Those not so good feelings of anger, fear, jealousy, guilt, and shame are valuable information as well. Those feelings are our EPS communicating to us that we have indeed taken a wrong turn and a change of direction is crucial. When we feel the emotions that don't feel good to us, our EPS is communicating that we must get off that particular road. There is a dead end ahead or even worse, a cliff that you are sure to fall off of if you proceed.

Our emotions communicate to us constantly. They provide us with data regarding whether or not you should pursue a degree in law to whether you should answer an incoming phone call. Let's say for instance your phone rings. You look at the caller ID and see that it is your friend Sandy calling. All of a sudden, there is a feeling of dread that comes over you. Stop and evaluate that emotion. Where is this emotion of dread stemming from? Is it dread regarding the conversation you anticipate or is this emotion directed toward Sandy, or is it both? Allow that emotion to surface and honor it. Utilize the data it is providing you with. Is this a friend who is constantly calling you with bad news, or to gossip or has conversation that is so negative in content that you are typically drained when you get off the phone with her? That feeling of dread that came over you is your EPS communicating to you that proceeding with the phone call is not advisable. Your EPS may be encouraging you to make a decision about that friendship. You may have to limit your conversations with her, insist that the conversation not be so negative in content or end that friendship altogether.

Let's say you are looking to buy a new home. You come across a home listing that seems perfect. The home is in a great neighborhood, the price is within your range and it has all the specifics you wanted. You make an appointment to go and see the home. From the outside, it looks perfect. You take a look inside and it appears to be well-maintained, has nice sized rooms and a floor plan that is to your liking. Based on all the specifics, this is the perfect home for you, but you can't seem to shake a feeling of discontent about the home. You try to talk yourself out of this emotion by reminding yourself how perfect the home is for you, but that gnawing emotion of discontent returns. Sometimes our EPS communicates to us through our intuition and at times our intuition is guiding us to make decisions we don't want to make. From the street level, the home looked perfect, but that gnawing feeling of discontent is your intuition communicating from the watchtower, seeing what you can't see, guiding you in the direction you should proceed in. From the intuitive watchtower your EPS is able to see all the potential pitfalls that owning that home would bring.

All emotions provide data as to your current emotional positioning and emotional positioning is a direct reflection of your success or lack thereof in your life. Use your EPS to intuitively communicate if you are proceeding in the right direction. The goal is to acknowledge all emotions both the good feeling and bad feeling ones. When you experience a not so good feeling emotion such as the ones listed below, your next move in life should be one that will lead you toward a more good feeling emotion. Like your GPS which provides you with the best route to take when moving toward a new destination, allow your EPS to activate the intuitive voice that will guide you toward your destination of success.

Good Feeling Emotions	Bad Feeling Emotions
Bliss	Boredom
Joy	Frustration
Love	Hate
Passion	Irritation
Happiness	Worry
Enthusiasm	Anger
Optimism	Pessimism
Hopefulness	Jealousy
Satisfaction	Rage
Excitement	Disappointment
Pride	Insecurity
Contentment	Guilt
Confidence	Fear
Connectedness	Loneliness
Appreciation	Despair

CHAPTER FOUR

STEP 4: VISUALIZATION

"Ordinary people believe only in the possible. Extraordinary people visualize not what is possible or probable, but rather what is impossible. And by visualizing the impossible, they begin to see it as possible."

~ Cherie Carter-Scott

By definition, visualization is the process of forming a mental picture of something. The concept of visualization is nothing new. Daydreaming, imagining and guided imagery are all forms of visualization. We have all engaged in visualization long before we could even pronounce the word. What we are now realizing is that we indeed hold the power to manipulate this process of visualization to achieve the things we want in life. The power that exists in visualization is no longer some unexplained mystical phenomenon that only an elite few can tap into. In the last several decades, it has become evident through scientific data that our brains play a pivotal role in not only formulating a visualization, but bringing it into reality as well.

A key component in this process is an area of the brain called the Reticular Activating System (RAS). Our RAS is sort of an information filtering system located at the base of our brain. It takes in all the trillions, yes, trillions of pieces of information we encounter day in and day out. Even information you aren't aware you are taking in is filtered by the RAS. For example, on your drive to work, you may pass hundreds even thousands of other vehicles. It is impossible to give conscious attention to all of those vehicles. That would be information overload. However, despite you not consciously paying attention to them, your RAS is taking in information about everything you come into contact with. You are not conscious to this process, but it is occurring. Your RAS decides if the information you are encountering in your daily comings and goings is relevant to you or not. When it is relevant, you are alerted and attend to that information. That which is not relevant to you is filtered out and discarded. Some people experience the process of the RAS after getting a new car and all of a sudden they begin noticing so many of the same model of car on the road. It isn't that an influx of these cars occurred after their purchase, it's simply that that particular car now holds relevance to them and thus they tune in to it, compliments of the RAS. Another example of the RAS at work is being at a cocktail party with numerous conversations going on at the same time. You could be across the room and not tuning into any of the particular conversations until you hear someone mention the name of a vacation destination you have desired traveling to. All of a sudden you tune in. Clear across the room you are alerted to this, compliments of your RAS and you begin to tune into the conversation, despite the 30 other conversations going on around you.

Simply put, our RAS alerts you when to tune in and when to turn off. The vast majority of information and data that you come into contact with on a daily basis you don't attend to, your RAS filters it out. However, when you encounter information that may be relevant to you or crucial to your survival, you tune in. You don't have to be told to tune in, it happens automatically without effort. It is your RAS that permits you to sleep through a thunderstorm, but awakens you to your crying baby. It is the RAS that filters all the noise and commotion on a crowded city street, but alerts you to a suspicious stranger to your right.

This RAS not only filters that which is relevant from that which is not, it is also goal seeking. Plant the seeds of your desires by visualizing them and your RAS will direct every one of your senses to be on alert to opportunities you encounter that can help make that vision a reality. So when you see, hear, smell, taste, touch or intuit something that may be instrumental in the realization of our desires, you will pay attention to it, therefore being tremendously less likely to allow an opportunity to slip through your fingers. Creating a visual representation of your desires through visualization gives your RAS the data it needs to alert you to an opportunity when it becomes available to you. It brings the desires of your heart to a rendezvous point in your reality.

Many Olympic and professional athletes have experienced the power of visualization in achieving their individual goals in their particular sport. Psychologists and visualization coaches are often brought in to engage the athlete in a guided visualization. The athletes are told to visualize themselves successfully engaging in their particular sport. They are guided through visualizing themselves excelling in their sport and overcoming any particular area of weakness that, in reality, may be preventing them from excelling. Athletes in baseball, basketball, golf, track & field, and every sport under the sun who have struggled with performance anxiety, poor batting averages, inability to make free throws, slumps in their golf game, etc. have taken advantage of the power of guided visualization to improve their athletic performance. Interestingly, when these athletes are engaging in this visualization, the same brain activity that would react if they had been actually engaging in that activity reacts during the visualization. This discovery lends evidence to the fact that the brain cannot distinguish between that which we are visualizing and that which is actually occurring in our reality. From a physiological perspective, our body reacts just the same. When we visualize something good, every cell in our body reacts accordingly releasing the feel good chemicals it would release if we had actually experienced that event. Conversely, when we visualize something bad, every cell in our body reacts accordingly, releasing all the stress chemicals that would be released if we were to actually experience that negative event. Visualization creates a dress rehearsal of the physiological processes that will occur in the actual achievement of the desire. This creates a pathway allowing for an easier manifestation of that which we visualize.

"For the thing that I fear comes to me."

~ Job 3:25

Visualizing yourself failing at an activity, arguing with your spouse, becoming ill with disease holds as much weight as visualizing yourself being successful in your endeavors, having a loving relationship and a healthy body. When we form a visual image of something, good or bad our RAS grabs to that visual image and begins to work to make it a reality. It doesn't matter if what you are visualizing is good or bad, with desirable or undesirable results, our brain is a goal seeking organism and once we plant the seed of intent with our particular visualization, our brain will work to make it a reality. The good news is that fleeting negative images which we all have from time to time don't inevitably become reality. The visualizations that we engage in most frequently are the ones that will have the greatest likelihood of manifesting into reality.

USING VISION BOARDS TO GET WHAT YOU WANT

Several years ago, after reading Jack Canfield's book *Success Principles* I developed my first *dream board*. Years later, while participating in a local prosperity class, I engaged in a process called *treasure mapping*. Some years after that, after watching the best selling DVD, *The Secret,* I created a vision board. In my quest toward learning the tools and practices that are inherent in creating a fulfilling, extraordinary life, I was repeatedly met by the concept of creating a physical representation of what I desired. Whether it was dream boards, treasure maps, or vision boards, it seemed that every success-oriented book and seminar I encountered touted the power that existed in placing visual images of the things you desire in your life on a tangible surface. It didn't matter if they were desires related to career, love, health or wealth, the theory was that creating a visual representation of those desires increased the likelihood of you attracting those very things to your life. As unscientific as this idea sounded, my active imagination, combined with a desire to test the validity of such an elementary concept motivated me to give it a try. I reasoned that I potentially had more to gain than to lose. The worst-case scenario would be that I'd have a colorful poster board of pictures and words that appealed to me to adorn my living space. Without much hesitation, I gathered a stack of old magazines, a poster board, scissors, a glue-stick and began construction of my first vision board.

"See things as you would have them be instead of as they are."

~ Robert Collier

My first vision board included pictures and words of the things I wanted to materialize in my life. Once completed, I placed my board on my dresser to ensure that I would be exposed to those images day and night. One item on my board was the words "increased finances." At that time I was studying for my licensing exam to become a fully licensed psychologist. The mountain of student loans as well as other debts accumulated over the years was taking its toll. I was working as an adjunct professor at one of the area colleges in addition to managing a small private practice. Any work opportunity that came along I grabbed it and as a result, I was spread thin between my work and family responsibilities. I placed power words such as "*abundance*" and "increased finances" on my board. I also included an image of a check made out to me with the figure of the salary I desired to make. I made it a practice to look at my board daily, day and night to ensure that the images were being transferred to my RAS and the seed of my desires would be firmly planted.

One important aspect of vision boards is to understand that you do not have to force your desires to materialize into reality. Once your intention is made, which is done by creating the board, that part of your brain, the RAS, will be working nonstop twenty-four hours, seven days a week to alert you to opportunities and practices that will make your desires a reality. In your waking hours and in your dream state, you will be alerted. In your waking hours, you will be tuned in, so when you encounter a person, situation, opportunity or thought that has the potential to make your vision a reality you will be alerted and not miss out on the opportunity. In some ways, your effort will be minimal in comparison to the effort your RAS will put forth. Even during your sleeping hours, you may have dreams that unexpectedly provide you with that ah-ha moment of insight that will direct you.

Within six months of creating my vision board, I passed my state boards. I received a phone call out of the blue from a former colleague of my sister. She informed me that the agency she worked for was looking for a licensed psychologist to perform contractual work. She went on to explain how the position was flexible and I could still maintain my private practice and part-time teaching at the college if I chose. Shortly thereafter, I interviewed for and was given the position which included a salary nearly twice as much as I had been earning.

I also had on my vision board a picture of an office space that was in a more desirable location than the office space I had. Specifically, I wanted office space located in the downtown area not far from the river and here's the kicker, I didn't want to pay for it. I wanted the space to be given to me. Months later, I received a call from a woman who had just opened a small private practice and needed supervision from a Ph.D. level licensed psychologist. The supervision required only a few hours of my time a month. The woman went on to explain that she didn't have the resources yet to reimburse me with money, but I could have full use of an office space that was located in the downtown area, just a block from the river.

Another item on my vision board was a picture of a private school that I wanted my sons to attend, but at nearly twenty thousand dollars per year per student, my reality did not support paying this type of money toward my boys' education. Although I had finished my doctoral program and passed my state exams, I was buried under a mountain of student loans and personal debt. I couldn't afford to send my boys to the school, but included the school on my vision board because it was my desire for them to attend.

A crucial requirement on vision board creation is to not convince yourself of the improbability of your desires. As you imagine and visualize the things you want for yourself, your mind will probably interfere with fears, doubts and disbelief. Your job is to not allow these fears, doubts or disbelief to influence what you include on your board. Don't limit your vision board to images and words that represent the potential that exists in your current reality. The idea with vision boards is to stretch your imagination beyond that which appears probable. Trust in the process even if you don't understand it and include on your vision board the things you genuinely desire. Go beyond your current reality.

Despite not being financially capable to send my sons to the school, I included the picture of the school on my vision board. When friends and family would visit my home and ask about that picture on my board I would tell them about the school, its philosophy and how I saw it as such a good fit for my children. Most would shrug their shoulders and seemingly not give it or my vision board a second thought. About a year after constructing the vision board, I received a phone call from a friend telling me she had met a woman who worked in the school's admissions department and informed her that one of the students who had been awarded a scholarship for the high school had to turn it down due to the student's family relocating out of state. The friend remembered seeing the picture of the school on my vision board, so when she met the woman who worked in the admissions department, she immediately thought of me. This friend's RAS tuned her in to information that could help make my desire a reality. I took the name and number of the woman in the admissions department and I followed up. As it turned out, the scholarship was for a person entering high school. It just so happened that my oldest son Aaron was entering the ninth grade at that time. After completing the application, Aaron was invited to interview with the school's admission department. With less than one month before the start of ninth grade, he was awarded a four-year scholarship to attend high school at the very school I had on my vision board.

Just prior to the start of his ninth grade year at the new school, our family attended a family orientation the school held. My youngest son, Ian, who had been playing the piano since the age of five, spotted a grand piano in the home the orientation was being held. As a kid who thoroughly enjoyed playing the piano, he couldn't resist the opportunity to get his fingers on the keys. After getting the permission of the homeowner, Ian jumped on the piano and begin to play. I witnessed the amazement on the faces of the other parents and school administrators who were probably expecting an elementary school rendition of "Twinkle, Twinkle Little Star" as opposed to an extremely sophisticated version of Beethoven's "Fir Elise." Ian received a round of applause and several compliments which was sufficient for him. A year and a half later, after Aaron had long adjusted to his new school environment, I received a call from the school admissions department indicating that there were scholarships available for incoming sixth graders and they were interested in my son, Ian, applying. As it turned out, Ian's performance at that orientation, nearly two years prior, resulted in an opportunity for him to apply and later be awarded a scholarship for all three years of middle school and the four years of high school.

Within a few years of creating my first vision board, the majority of the items had indeed manifested into reality. I decided it was time to create another vision board. My life had changed radically since I had created the first board. I was now a divorced, single parent of four. My career had began to take off. I had developed the seven step process and witnessed firsthand how it was transforming the lives of others. The desire to share this with larger audiences was strong. In my second vision board I included the desire to increase my speaking opportunities. I had so many extraordinary experiences from incorporating the seven step process in my life and so many of my clients were reaching out to share their experiences that I knew I needed to reach more people. On my second vision board, I included pictures of microphones to represent speaking. I included power words such as 'networking' and 'opportunity.' I also included a picture of Oprah Winfrey because she represented the ultimate opportunity that existed for visibility. Like millions of other women and men, I had been trying for years to get tickets to be part of The Oprah Winfrey Show's studio audience without success. Less than a year after completing my second vision board I saw an advertisement from one of the local TV news stations looking for entries into an Oprah's Biggest Fan contest to kick off her twenty-fourth season. Contestants would be required to write an essay not to exceed 100 words on why they are Oprah's biggest fan. My understanding was that the winner would have a local chef come to their home to prepare dinner for the winner and ten guests as they watched the season opener of the Oprah Winfrey Show.

As a fan since my teenage years, I thought it would be cool to host a dinner party at my home to watch her season opener, but my ultimate goal was to meet her one day, so my motivation and urgency to enter the essay contest was admittedly not high. One day before the contest deadline, I received a call from a childhood friend who knew of my admiration for Oprah and my love of writing. She asked if I was going to enter the contest. I told her I had considered it but hadn't entered. She talked about how fun a dinner party would be and we shifted the conversation to other topics. That night, I went to bed, but could not sleep. I kept thinking about the contest and how refreshing a catered dinner party with friends would be after coming out of a tumultuous couple of years that included divorce and financial difficulty. I got out of bed at one o'clock in the morning and began writing an essay of why I considered myself Oprah's biggest fan. Anyone who has a passion for writing knows how difficult it can be to express yourself in 100 words or less. After over two hours of tweaking, deleting, and modifying, I finally got the essay down to 100 words exactly. The essay read as follows:

After my fairly new laptop started moving sluggishly, I took it to the repair shop. After checking it out the tech laughingly stated, "Your problem is that you have too many Oprah shows saved on your system."

He went on to add, "We'll need to erase them to speed your system up."

I had been Tivo-ing Oprah for nearly 10 years and transferring the shows to my laptop. Erasing was not an option. I instead granted my "O-book, notebook" a stay of execution and *purchased an entirely separate system. There are some things a girl just can't part with.*

I filled out the contest application, attached my essay and with just hours before the deadline I hit the submit button. One week later, I received a call from a producer with the local news station informing me that I was the winner. My prize, as I expected, was a catered party in my home for ten of my closest friends. To my surprise, the prize also included an all expense paid trip to the Oprah Winfrey Show to be part of the studio audience!

Six weeks after having a catered dinner party broadcast over the local news station I was standing outside of Harpo Studios getting ready to be part of the studio audience. As surreal as the experience of stepping inside Harpo Studios was, I was committed to soak it all in. Too often, when an item on our vision board becomes a reality we will miss out on a great deal of that experience because our excitement gets the best of us. I made a point of consciously taking in every detail of the experience from waiting in line in the wee hours of the morning to sitting in the holding room with the other 299 audience members waiting to take our seat. What occurred over the next hour of that live taping further supported the power of vision boards and will be elaborated on in the next chapter on affirmations.

HOW TO MAKE A VISION BOARD

Your personal vision board should be a reflection of you. The vision boards created by my students, clients and workshop participants are just as diverse as they are. I have had students choose poster boards that they may later frame, foam core boards or cork-boards. Others have displayed their images in elaborate shadow boxes that they will hang on their wall. More recently, several clients have turned to technology and constructed vision board screen savers utilizing one of the many online applications for constructing vision boards.

I recently had a client contact me to tell me just twenty-four hours after constructing a vision board online and making it his screen saver, a goal that had eluded him his entire adult life was achieved. An avid bowler for over thirty years, he had never been able to bowl a perfect game. He had played on numerous leagues over the years and considered himself to be a good bowler, but he could never capture that 300 score. After listening to a radio program I was on discussing the power of vision boards, he decided to give it a try. Among other items, he included the words "300 Score" with a picture of bowling pins beneath. The next night he met with his bowling league. Just prior to the start of the first game he said to himself, "I am bowling a perfect game tonight." He proceeded to make one strike right after another. He shared how the experience seemed so surreal and how the bowling alley seemed to become still as he let go of his last ball in the tenth frame. When he witnessed all ten pins scatter, he reports standing there in amazement as people in the bowling alley erupted in applause. He was convinced in the power of vision boards that night and makes it a point to look at his vision board screen saver daily.

Despite the inevitable variation that will exist in vision boards, they all should include:

Visual Representations. Make your vision board as visual as possible with pictures to represent the items you want to manifest in your reality. You can and should also supplement your images with words that depict your desires as my bowling client did. Your RAS likes visual images to grab hold to. Adding words or phrases will provide a more powerful representation.

Emotional Appeal. Looking at your vision board should elicit positive emotional responses from you. Your vision board should ignite and motivate your passion to make those images a reality.

Every time I looked at the vibrant picture of Hawaii that I included on my second vision board, a sense of serenity would rush through me. The colorful flowers and waterfall leading into a stream surely elicited a feel good response from me. I had always wanted to visit the island and witness firsthand the beauty that so many rave about. So I decided to include it on my vision board. For the first time on my vision board I included a date under an image. My desire was to manifest a Hawaiian vacation by the date I indicated. That date came and left with no Hawaii. I did not remove the image. I simply accepted that the timing was not right. I did not try to force it. I simply left the Hawaiian visual image on my board and relished in it. About a year later I received a phone call from my sister asking if I was interested in traveling to Hawaii with her.

She indicated that she and her husband had planned to go, but at the last minute he had to back out. She went on to explain that all I needed to do was pay for airfare. The resort was already paid for. Four weeks later I was waking up in Maui to sunrises over the Pacific Ocean.

Flexibility in Timing. It is not recommended that you include a due date on your images as I did with my Hawaii image. You must trust that if the image is in your best interest and in alignment with what is best for you, it will happen when it is supposed to. You risk extinguishing your motivation and passion toward your images if you bombard your board with due dates.

Location, Location, Location. Choose a location for your board that will increase your exposure to it. Placing it in a room that you rarely enter is not giving your RAS the regular exposure it needs to your images. Regular exposure to your vision board creates an energy that increases the chances and decreases the time it takes to manifest your desires. Bedrooms and bathrooms are a great location. My sister-in-law has her vision board prominently displayed in her dining room providing her exposure to it every mealtime. I have had clients to express concern regarding the possibility of being criticized or even ridiculed by others for making a vision board. Many will express purposely storing their vision boards in closets or under their beds to avoid judgment. If this is your concern, understand that being overly concerned with the opinions of others is a surefire way of blocking your desires from coming into reality. Negative judgment or criticism about your vision board can stifle the energy required to allow it to materialize, but only if you allow it. Over the years, the materialization of many of my desires that were on my vision boards have convinced many skeptics. It is a regular occurrence for me to receive phone calls or emails from family and friends, who once laughed at the prominent display of my vision boards in my home excitedly sharing with me how they have just finished their first vision board.

Recommended Supplies: Board Surface, Magazines, Stencils, Markers, Computer/Printer, Scissors, Creativity

Vision board surface. This may include: Poster board, foam core board, tri-fold cardboard or tri-fold core board, cork board, shadow box, etc.

Magazines. You will cut out the pictures, words and phrases that you will include on your board. It is best to have a large assortment of magazines to choose from.

Stencils/Markers. If there is a particular phrase that you want to include on your board (ex. "Carpe Diem") and you can't locate it in a magazine, feel free to stencil or write it on your vision board or print it from your computer.

Computer/Printer. You can also search images and phrases on the Internet to print out and use.

Glue. Use glue sticks to affix your images and words.

Scissors. Cut out images and words from various magazines to apply to your board.

Creativity. What you ultimately choose to include on your vision board is entirely up to you. You want to choose images that have relevance and significance to you. A picture of a child on your board may represent your desire to bring out the kid in you whereas, it may represent another person's desire for a child. It is more important that your images and phrases have significance to you than universal appeal.

CHOOSE, REMOVE, PLACE, PASTE

Step 1 - **Choose.** Select the pictures, phrases and words you want to include on your vision board. Choose from magazines, Internet searches or visuals you've found at your local craft store. Doing Internet searches or going to a craft store to find pictures can save time because in comparison to magazines that may not have the exact image you desire, you are able to be specific in your Internet search, typing the word of the image you are seeking and having plenty of choices to choose from. You can also go directly to the area in the craft store that represents your desires. If you desire traveling, there exists an entire section, usually in the scrapbooking area that will have a large selection of images to choose from. A client of mine brought her vision board to one of our sessions and I was completely blown away at how visually appealing it was. In addition to magazine and Internet pictures, she went to the local craft store and found colorful three-dimensional cut outs to include on her board. One of her desires was to fall in love and get married. She went to the wedding section of the craft shop and purchased scrap book appliqués of items related to weddings. The images were not only relevant to her goals but elicited the emotional response of excitement and joy. Be sure your images are a direct match to your imagination.

Step 2 - **Remove.** Cut out all of your selected images, phrases and words from the magazines. Print and cut out all the images and words derived from your Internet search. If there are appliqués you are adding to your board, place them with your magazine and Internet items. Now that you have all the potential items in front of you, spend some time selecting the images that you most want to include on your board. Often times we will cut out and select way more images that will fit on our boards. Once you place all of your options in front of you, you are better able to make a decision of what you will ultimately include.

Step 3 - **Place.** Don't start gluing items as you cut them out. It is best to first arrange your pictures on your board. Arrange them in a way that is visually appealing to you and resonates those feel good emotions you want to evoke whenever you look at your board. Perhaps the desire you most want to happen in your life takes center stage on your board. You may decide to organize the things you want to happen career-wise in one particular area on the board and place your health and relationship desires in a separate area on the board. You may ultimately decide to mix it all up and place your items randomly on your board to symbolize how you want all the areas of focus to integrate with each other. Whatever approach you choose is fine as long as it holds relevance to you.

Step 4 - **Paste.** Now that you have arranged your board in a manner that is best-suited for you, you can start pasting the images in place. Utilize glue (for poster/foam core boards) or pins (for cork boards, shadow boxes). Once your images are secure and in place you can proudly hang your vision board in your chosen location and allow the manifestation to begin!

UPDATING YOUR VISION BOARD

After nearly eight years since developing my first vision board I am on my third board. It had gone from a tri-fold core board to a poster board to currently a shadow box. As time passes and your life transforms you may find your desires have changed as well. As the items on your vision board are achieved or your desires change, you may choose to update your board with new images. Depending on how many of those items have manifested or how much your life may have changed, you may choose to construct an entirely new vision board. Life is not static, nor should your vision board be. Your vision board should always remain an accurate, current reflection of the things you want to happen in your life.

CHAPTER FIVE

STEP 5: AFFIRMATIONS

"I am the greatest, I said that even before I knew I was."

~ Muhammad Ali

Florence Scovel Shinn was a metaphysical teacher in the early 1900s. A visionary ahead of her time, her 1940 book, *Mind, Body, Spirit*, indicated that you will be a failure, until you impress upon your subconscious mind the conviction that you are a success. According to Shinn, this is accomplished by making affirmations. Some may think references to the subconscious mind and the power we have to transform our lives through words as a novel, new age concept, born in the self-help movement of the latter part of the twentieth century and satirized in comedies (a la *Saturday Night Live's* Stuart Smiley character). However, the power that exists in the utilization of affirmations has a very long history indeed. From the Bible, to the Koran, to the teachings of Buddha, references to the power of affirmations have been found in the earliest writings known to man. The burning bush story in the Bible discusses Moses asking God what His name is and God replying "I Am that I Am." It is easy to see how that simple phrase "I am" can be glossed over by readers as insignificant, yet these two seemingly insignificant words, are two of the most powerful words known to mankind. When you preface any statement with "I am" you are in fact summoning action by speaking what follows that phrase into existence. "I am" speaks to the highest power that resides within you, your God consciousness. Plainly stated, your "I am" statement is the reality you have and are creating for yourself. Affirmations have the power to give strength to elements within ourselves that will allow us to transform. Affirmations also have the power to give strength to elements within ourselves that will keep us in a state of unfulfillment and stagnation. Affirmations are power. How we harness its power is completely up to us.

Thomas was a 43 year-old male client that I had been treating for a few months. He initially came to me with an overwhelming sense of stagnation and a lack of motivation. He had gotten so far behind in his work responsibilities that he feared being fired. At home, his lack of motivation to complete projects in the home he and his wife were renovating was creating problems in his marriage. He presented to me a laundry list of his shortcomings and the barriers that stood in the way of him being successful including weight, financial, and self-esteem difficulties. In this particular session I gave him the assignment to write down five affirmations and to speak the affirmations aloud morning, noon and night. Thomas respectfully laughed at my suggestion.

"No offense, Doc," he shared, "but this idea of reciting affirmations is a bit out of my comfort zone. It just seems plain goofy."

There was no offense taken in Thomas' comment. In fact, I had heard it before from other clients who initially didn't see any value or connection between affirmations and goal achievement. I did however challenge Thomas' statement, asking him how could he say such a thing considering he had just passionately stated five affirmations to me in the course of our fifty minute session without me even asking. Thomas gave a look of confusion. Before he could challenge me, I scrolled back in my notepad and repeated the five affirmations he had stated during our session.

"I am so tired."
"I am broke."
"I am never going to get out of this jam."
"I am so frustrated over the entire project."
"I am probably going to lose my wife over this one."

Thomas' eyes widened, realizing for the first time that the words he so often spoke were exactly the opposite of what he wanted in his life. I instructed him to consider the words he spoke, especially the words he prefaced with "I am," as constant requests being made to whatever higher power he believed in. Many of us have become so accustomed to unconsciously sending out constant requests of exactly what we don't want. Somewhere along the line we started to engage regularly in accentuating the negative, foolishly hoping that doing so will bring about the exact opposite. That skewed thinking is what has so many of us caught in this vicious cycle of getting exactly what we don't want over and over again.

In the phenomenal DVD *The Secret*, affirmations are likened to placing an order. When you are in a restaurant and order a nice juicy steak, you expect the waiter to bring you precisely what you order, right? Imagine going to a restaurant and ordering that choice cut of steak with all the trimmings and having the waiter bring back a plate of spaghetti. You would be up in arms, sending the meal back and demanding you get the food you requested. Yet, day in and day out you continue to order a life of lack, limitation, poverty and loneliness expecting to get back abundance, opportunity and fulfilling relationships. This defies law. What you affirm, you confirm.

Truth is, we all utilize affirmations in our daily lives, the problem is most of the affirming we do is counterproductive due to the negative content of most of our default affirmations. Not only do people fail to realize they are using affirmations regularly in their lives, but they fail to realize that they are using them to maintain their current state of despair. Unbeknownst to them, they have this default setting for using affirmations—powerful "I am" statements that add no value to their lives.

Just as possible as it is for positive things to occur through affirmation, it must be understood that negative affirmations have just as much of a chance of coming true. In fact, it can be argued that negative affirmations actually tend to manifest more quickly than positive ones because we usually express the negative ones with more feeling and conviction than positive ones thus giving them more energy to form. It is that element of emotion and conviction you express your affirmation with that typically allows it to take shape. Over the years, I have found that the people speaking their affirmations with the most emotion are precisely the ones whose lives are evident with no uncertain terms that which they have affirmed.

People who profess "I am broke" are usually stating it with such passion and vigor that they can't help but to receive a double order of "brokeness." So not only have they encountered an unexpected car repair, but their employer has just announced a 10 percent pay cut. People who are always professing how sick and tired they are never appear to get well or achieve vitality. Women who insist in heated conversations with their girlfriends that there are no good men around will continue to attract countless men who will see to it that their affirmation is confirmed, time after time. The emotion you put behind your affirmation is like a turbo boost, giving that affirmation even more power.

Your connection with the "I am" is infinite, unlimited and precise. You have the choice of using the affirmative power of these two words to manifest success in your life or utilize it to elicit circumstances, situations and events that you don't want. I am continually amazed at the power of affirmations in my own life. The things that manifest in our life, both the good and the bad are confirmation that there is power in our words.

I AM meeting Oprah Winfrey, I AM talking with Oprah Winfrey

After winning tickets to the Oprah Winfrey Show I awaited for the big day of being part of the studio audience. As opposed to spending the week leading up to my visit in anxious anticipation, I spent a great deal of that week professing affirmations that were consistent with my desire to meet and speak with Oprah one day. I walked around my home repeatedly affirming, "I am talking with Oprah. I am meeting Oprah. I am taking a picture with Oprah." My four children would look at me with the look of *"enough already"* as I repeatedly made these affirmations with so much conviction and excitement that you would have thought it was happening right in that moment.

A week later, I was in Chicago, Illinois at Harpo Studios awaiting the beginning of the show. Just being there in the studio was fulfilling a twenty year desire to be in the studio audience. Prior to the live taping, show producers engaged audience members by asking our critique of the Michael Jackson's *This is It* movie we had viewed the night before. Audience member after audience member including myself shared reflections of the movie as we passed time waiting for the show to begin. I soaked in the environment and relished in the fact that one of my long-term desires had indeed manifested.

Eventually, the moment we all awaited arrived. The Queen of Talk herself walked out on stage and the live taping began. It was surreal to watch this living legend enter the room. She took her seat, cameras began to roll and she commenced to doing what she does best. She shared how the 300 audience members all previewed the movie the night before. She shared her own reflections of the movie. Then, without warning, Oprah Winfrey looked directly at me during the live taping and said, "You had something to say." Stunned, I had a look on my face as if to ask, "Me?" She responded, "Yes, you, stand up." In a live taping, in front of 32 million people around the world, I went on to engage in a dialogue with Oprah Winfrey regarding the transcendent power of the movie. Out of the 300 audience members, I was the only member she chose to speak with about the movie.

"I am talking with Oprah."

I was still floating on cloud nine when the show ended. As audience members waited to exit the studio, one of the staff members came out and asked me and my guest to follow her backstage. As we walked, she turned to us and announced, "You are going backstage to meet and take a picture with Oprah."

"I am meeting Oprah."

"I am taking a picture with Oprah."

The power of affirmations was reinforced exponentially for me that day. I knew without question that it was my persistent and vehement affirmation that garnered me the opportunity to engage in dialogue and take a picture with the woman that I and millions of others around the world admired.

What are you affirming on a regular basis regarding your health, wealth and relationships? If you are like most, you are either not utilizing affirmations or unknowingly engaging in affirmations that won't lead you to the life you deserve or desire. Create a list of affirmations for yourself that empowers the most important areas of your life such as health, wealth and love.

List 10 Daily Affirmations for Yourself Using the Power of
***I Am*:**

1. I am _____ .
2. I am _____ .
3. I am _____ .
4. I am _____ .
5. I am _____ .
6. I am _____ .
7. I am _____ .
8. I am _____ .
9. I am _____ .
10. I am _____ .

Make a practice of reciting these affirmations daily. Use affirmations to affirm your daily intent as well as short and long term desires. Depending on what is going on in your life, you may choose to focus your affirmation more in that particular area. For example, if you have a surgery scheduled, you may choose to create the following affirmation, "I am rejoicing in my successful surgery." Perhaps you have a major exam coming up, you may choose to spend the weeks or days leading up to your exam affirming, "I am answering the questions correctly on my exam." Affirmations can be recited anytime of the day. You may choose to affirm your intentions first thing in the morning or during your morning drive. You may choose to speak your affirmations before going to bed at night. The choice is yours. Affirmations should be done daily. It doesn't hurt to speak them several times throughout the day, whenever the urge hits you. As stated before, it is imperative that you conjure emotions when reciting your affirmations. Emotions such as joy, bliss, enthusiasm, pride, relief and passion should be experienced as you say your affirmations. Feel the emotions that you would expect to feel when the very thing you are affirming becomes reality.

USE AFFIRMATIONS IN CONJUNCTION WITH YOUR VISION BOARD

Once you have completed your vision board, you may choose to develop a list of affirmations to correlate with the items on your board. So if you have a picture of a graduation cap to represent you completing an educational goal, write an affirmation that correlates to the image. "I am walking across the stage receiving my diploma."

One of the biggest mistakes people make that creates resistance in the manifestation of the items on their vision board is speaking language that is inconsistent with what is on their board. For example, you have a picture of the home of your dreams on your board, but in your daily conversation you affirm how you will never be able to afford a home like that. Or you have a visual representation of being a world traveler on your vision board, yet speak of how that dream vacation is out of your league, your price range, how your boss would never approve the time, etc. Conversations and beliefs that negate your desires for yourself will block any forward movement, each and every time. Take care that the conversation you engage in with others is consistent with your affirmations. This creates an vibrational energy of non-resistance.

Discover what millions of successful people have discovered regarding affirmations. Affirmations are key to developing the power necessary for personal transformation. Affirmations in conjunction with visualization can transform your life, your health, your relationships and ignite the joy and passion that gives life meaning.

Affirmations on Rediscovering You

I am true to my authentic self

I am expressing the true essence of who I am

I am rediscovering me

I am constantly evolving and becoming more conscious of self

I am trusting God's plan for me

I am self-motivated

I am talented and possess all the skills I need to be successful

I am a reflection of the people I desire to attract in my life

I am living by my own standards

I am loving, trusting and appreciating myself

Affirmations on C.A.L.M.S. ~ Living in the Now

I am content and comfortable in the present moment

I am in control of my thinking

I am embracing the here and now

I am able to return to the present moment when my focus shifts to past or future

I am using thinking only for planning and strategy

I am challenging limiting beliefs and replace them with affirming ones

I am free from compulsive thinking

I am challenging what I have always regarded as truth and embracing the truth that validates me

I am accepting all life's experiences and recognize the value in pleasant and unpleasant situations

I am calm and connected to the present

Affirmations on Making Sense of Your Senses

I am tuned into my senses and allow them to guide and direct me

I sense my body in all activities I engage in, be it eating, cooking, cleaning, etc.

I am able to see the truth in everyone I meet

I watch my feelings and emotions and allow them to guide me

As I trust my intuitive feelings and act on them I feel powerful and alive

I am activating my birthright of intuition

I am thankful and value the beauty I witness in daily life

I am highly intuitive and I follow my intuitive guidance daily

I can easily distinguish my intuitive voice from my ego

I am accessing my sixth sense easily and it delivers simple and straightforward messages

Affirmations on Visualization

I am planting the seeds of my desires

Whatever I visualize, I materialize

I am a magnet attracting unto myself

I am passionate enough to make my visions a reality

I am allowing the manifestation of my vision

I am creating a mental image of my desired result

I am clear in my vision and recognize opportunities that will bring my vision into reality

I manipulate my perceived limitations with the unlimited possibilities of my vision

I am seeing my success even before it materializes

I am expediting my goals through visualization and affirmations

Affirmations on Meditation/Stillness

I am comfortable in silence

I am restored through stillness

I find strength and clarity in stillness

I am transformed through stillness

Meditation connects me to the infinite wisdom of the universe

I achieve clarity through meditation

I am in vibrational alignment with the universe

I am open to receive my desires

I am raising my vibrational frequency

I am open to receive divine guidance

Affirmations on Connectedness

I am attracting to myself that which I desire

I will not lower my vibration to connect to another

I recognize the connection between my thoughts and my outcome

I am connecting to the reality that is consistent with my desires

I am connected

I am plugged into the natural flow of the universe

I am raising my vibrational energy

I am connecting with positive individuals

Connectedness is the theme song of my life

I see how the past, present and future connect

CHAPTER SIX

STEP 6: STILLNESS

"Stillness is where creativity and solutions to problems are
formed."
~ Eckhart Tolle

For many, the start of a new day is met with an exasperated sigh. Before you have a chance to open your eyes, or even focus them for that matter, the demands of life grab you. Your daily routine begins in a hurried state bordering mania. In a panic, you wonder if the kids have clean clothes. Is there enough bread to make lunch? Is the homework in the backpack? Is there enough gas in the car? During your struggle through rush hour traffic you question if you remembered to leave a check for the lawn service.

By the time you make it to work you're worn out, but dare not think about resting. You must switch over to worker mode before the boss passes by. You spend the day on the phone with disgruntled customers. You can't seem to locate an important file. Just as you are putting the finishing touches on the quarterly report for the 10 a.m. meeting, the computer system goes down. At lunchtime you inhale a sandwich, chase it down with a big gulp of water and spend the last fifteen minutes at lunch scheduling doctors' appointments for the family and paying a few bills online. By 1 p.m. you're back on the grind, working nonstop until it's time to pick up the kids. During your commute you switch back and forth between your email inbox that's overflowing to the empty box of cereal at home. You detour to the grocery store before picking up the kids.

On autopilot you make it home, whip up a decent meal, do a load of laundry while helping with homework. You're spelling t-r-u-c-k, stirring rice and adding fabric softener simultaneously. You bathe the kids, tell them a story, finish an assignment for the online class you're taking. By the time you sit down and exhale, it's past bedtime. You take your shower, appreciative of finally having time to yourself. You shower so quickly that you don't give the water a chance to reach full pressure. You dive into bed and your spouse nudges you. Exhausted, you dig deep, deep inside to find that button, the one that switches you into being that ever giving, devoted, attentive, dynamic, full-of-energy lover. Sleep eventually overpowers the intrusive thoughts you have about finding time to get your hair cut, the car washed, your annual physical and...RIIIING!!! The alarm clock awakens you to start the entire process all over again.

To some degree we can all relate to this scenario. Think about your day from the time you awoke until now. Consider all the details in your day that required your attention. Try to recall them all, even the ones you consider insignificant. Our days are filled with constant movement, demands and requirements that distract us from connecting to stillness. Even as I sat to begin writing this chapter on stillness, several mini-crises required attention. My oldest son called from college to inform me there was a financial hold on his college account due to a banking error. My daughter needed my assistance on a school project that was due the next day. My youngest daredevil fell off her skateboard, a feat that subsequently required a search for peroxide and bandages. As the evening progressed, I fulfilled my promise to the girls by reading them a never-ending Dr. Seuss book. It worked like a charm... at putting me to sleep. When I finally jarred myself out of my premature slumber to retreat to my desk, I realized that dinner had not been put away, the towels were still in the washing machine and someone had spilled animal crackers all over the kitchen floor.

As I spent the next half hour tidying things up and sweeping the last graham-flavored giraffe off the floor, I laughed at the irony of how the most challenging part of writing this chapter on stillness was finding the time to be still. Before I could even attempt to involve myself in my pursuit to finish this chapter, I had to slow down, like a plane descending. I had to shift from perpetual motion, decelerate from moving at the speed of 1,000 miles per hour and allow my eardrums to adjust from the constant vibration of movement to the gentle sound of stillness that will welcome the words I want to communicate.

"We teach what we most need to learn."
~ Richard Bach

Stillness has always eluded me. Like most, I had gotten in the habit of allowing life to grab me even before I left my bed in the morning. From the moment my feet were planted firmly on the floor, the starter gun was fired and like a marathon, I was off. We live in a time when multitasking and being on the constant go is regarded a badge of honor. Stillness is a distant cousin that we've lost contact with. Our moments of stillness are garnered haphazardly, say for instance, when we have been unexpectedly delayed. Traffic, flight and appointment delays are seen as inconveniences and are often met with passionate protests. Moments of stillness are not intentionally sought, for such an act may be regarded as laziness. I'm reminded of how there was a time in which I actually looked forward to one of the most dreaded appointments of all, the dentist appointment. Sitting in that examination chair in the dentist office would likely be the first moment of stillness I had experienced in weeks. I would actually relish the relaxation in the dentist's chair as I listened to the soothing music playing over the intercom system. It was not uncommon for me to grab a rare, quick nap as I waited for the dentist to enter the room.

Like many women, I was raised to be superwoman with a capital "S." I watched my predecessor and her predecessor perform superhuman feats. It was always the expectation that I would not only learn, but embrace juggling the many responsibilities that seemed to come with being a woman, mother, wife and worker. Growing up, many of us heard testimony after testimony of how Grandma raised thirteen kids and how easy she made the job seem. *"That household ran like a well-oiled machine."* As a young girl it sounded so easy, so natural, so enticing and appealing. Now, generations later, many women like myself are realizing that perhaps we weren't told the whole truth. Or perhaps we chose to only focus on the elements of womanhood that were consistent with the fairy tale idea that was spoon-fed to us. Or maybe we failed to take into account that in addition to equal rights which propelled us into the workforce, we were still expected to maintain all our other roles with their never-ending description of duties.

My practice is filled with multi-roled, multi-tasking women who come to me feeling disillusioned and disenfranchised, like someone pulled the wool over their eyes. And now that they've removed the rose-colored glasses, they're finally getting a firsthand look at the truth. The not-so-pretty-sometimes-very-ugly-truth. Following one of my seminars, a wife and mother of two approached me to share how my discussion on this topic resonated with her. She indicated that she suffered with a chronic illness that is generally well managed. However, she went on to share with a look of embarrassment that a part of her secretly looked forward to the times her illness would flare up because she sees the few days she spends in the hospital as an opportunity and excuse to be take a break from all of her daily responsibilities.

"My day is managed on autopilot. After awakening from the few hours of sleep I do get, I think I just zone out as I start getting the kids and myself together."
~ Krystal, mother of two

Common sense tells us not to leave a battery-operated device on all day, not to overload an outlet with plugs or not to leave a light bulb on unnecessarily. We are all aware of the consequences in these scenarios. The batteries run down, the fuse blows, and the little filament in the light bulb burns away. This is where we stand today. We are running down our battery, blowing our fuses and burning away the filament of sanity. Millions of women and men in today's society are in crisis, and that crisis is one of constant motion. By far, the majority of the people I encounter who can relate to this epidemic do consider it problematic. They regard the change, frustration and pressure that accompanies their daily demands as a major stressor. From a physiological standpoint, our bodies were not designed to endure chronic stressors. Chronic stress taxes our bodies and it's a tax we can't afford to pay.

Most of us are familiar with the fight-or-flight response. Even if you aren't familiar with the terminology you've had firsthand experience of fight-or-flight at work. It is the physical reaction that happens when we are faced with a frightening or threatening situation. Whenever we encounter a potentially harmful or threatening situation, several physiological reactions occur. Our hearts beat faster (this is so more blood will be pumped to our large muscles preparing us to fight or flee for our lives). Our mouths' become dry (saliva glands are inhibited). Our digestion slows down (your body does not want to expend energy digesting a meal when you need to fight or run) and breathing becomes shallow (abdominal muscles contract to protect our internal organs from attack). Our adrenal glands also saturate our bodies with adrenaline to provide an instant and powerful source of energy. All these responses serve the purpose of protecting and preparing us. This fight-or-flight phenomenon has been around since the beginning of man and served its purpose well in human evolution when imminent danger was more frequent.

Thankfully, most of us are not faced with life threatening situations on a daily basis in which we must decide whether to fight or flee. This is not to say, however, that this system is being underutilized. To the contrary, some argue that the fight-or-flight response is being activated more today than it was when we had to fight off hungry dinosaurs. Anytime you perceive something as a threat, like having to speak publicly, being caught in traffic or overwhelmed at work, your coping abilities are taxed. You send a signal to your glands telling them there is danger. Those glands alert your organs. As a result, your heart, lungs, intestines, pancreas, etc. begin to respond out of the norm. If you continue this routine of interpreting your life as being stressful and overwhelming on a daily basis it will wear and wreak havoc on your organs and your immune system, making you more susceptible to disease. Researchers in health psychology recognize the connection to our hectic lifestyles and the development of disease. In our grandparents' and great-grandparents' time it was contagious diseases that were the leading causes of death in our society. In modern day society however, it is chronic diseases like congestive heart failure, diabetes, and hypertension that are among the leading causes. By definition, chronic illness takes time to develop. High stress, high movement lifestyles are fertile ground for disease. Many people are unaware that each and every day you rob yourself of the restorative power of stillness you are increasing the likelihood that you will develop a debilitating illness. So, the non-stop movement, the multi-tasking, the wearing of twenty different hats on a daily basis has the potential to kill you.

STILLNESS RESTORES AND RECHARGES

If your life is like mine, there is no way of getting around many of the responsibilities you face daily. Parenting, work, family and household responsibilities are in of themselves chronic. It would be illogical to think you could totally free yourself of all your responsibilities, just as it would be illogical to believe you can live a stress-free life. It is however, not only possible, but absolutely imperative for you to learn to control and ultimately eliminate the devastating effects of your busy lifestyle.

Achieving stillness is possible for all. As you sit in a place of stillness you find the strength to just let things be. As you surrender to stillness you discover a place of acceptance. Through this acceptance you develop the capacity to handle and rise above whatever life may bring you. Stillness opens your mind and bypasses all those cluttered thoughts. It lets you see things from an objective view point. The stillness brings a state of pure awareness and calm. This is where you find the power to release fears and begin living from a positive place of strength, clarity, and love for yourself.

ACHIEVING STILLNESS THROUGH BREATHING AND MEDITATION

Breathing

Breathing sustains life. It is one of those physiological processes that we don't give much thought to because its automatic, seemingly not requiring any attention. However, studies have estimated that as many as eighty percent of adults do not breathe properly. When you don't breathe properly, it is impossible to feel well. Most of us take for granted the automatic process of breathing. We regard breathing as we do other physiological processes that occur without our influence, like our hearts beating and our kidneys filtering. The fact is, however, that most people have unconsciously altered their breathing, breathing in ways that block their ability to get the full benefit of it. Proper breathing improves mood, reduces fatigue and helps you better manage the daily demands of life, thus minimizing the mental and physical effects of stress.

Midway through my seven steps to personal transformation workshops, participants are asked to close their eyes as I engage them in a relaxation exercise. Truth is, the primary purpose of this exercise is to evaluate the participants' breathing. As I stroll the room observing their breath patterns, it becomes obvious that most are engaging in improper breathing. Most adults breathe with tense stomach muscles, resulting in breathing that is too fast or too shallow. This tension prevents the lungs from fully expanding and forces the breath into their chests. As I walk around the workshop room observing breathing patterns, I observe significantly more chest breathers than stomach breathers. When you can see a person's shoulders rise up and go down, or their chest raise and decline it is a tell-tale sign that their breathing is off. Proper breathing can be observed in babies. As babies breathe, their stomach muscles remain relaxed and the stomach muscles rises with each inhalation. Infants pull their entire breath in all the way to the bottom of their lungs as they inhale and slowly exhale the full breath.

The main reason an estimated eighty percent of people don't breathe properly is because of stress factors. As discussed earlier, when a situation is interpreted as stressful, it triggers the fight-or-flight response resulting in increased heart rates, contraction of abdominal muscles causing our breathing to speed up and move up into our chests. In a Johns Hopkins University study, researchers went into waiting rooms of doctors' offices to observe the breathing patterns of patients as they awaited their appointment. Nearly 90 percent of the patients, regardless of the illness they were suffering from, exhibited improper breathing patterns. The more intriguing question that researchers are now studying is what came first, the improper breathing or the various ailments the patients suffered with. I think we can all agree that there is ample evidence to support the detriment that exists with improper breathing. The focus now must shift to reaping the enormous benefits of proper breathing patterns.

HOW TO BREATHE PROPERLY

1. Lie on your back on a flat surface or sit comfortably in a chair with your feet planted on the floor. Place one hand on your upper chest and the other hand on your diaphragm, just below your rib cage.
2. As you breathe slowly through your nose your stomach should move out against your hand. Allow your stomach to push your hand out as far as possible as you inhale. The hand on your chest should remain perfectly still.

3. As you slowly exhale through your mouth, your stomach with your hand still on top should fall inward. Slowly allow the entire breath to exhale. Repeat three times.

It is recommended you practice this exercise daily as you retrain yourself to breathe properly. You may also choose to place a book on your stomach (instead of your hand) when you lay down to practice this exercise. The book will serve as an indicator as to whether you are breathing properly. As you inhale, the book should rise. As you exhale, it will return back to its starting position.

SQUARE BREATHING

Square breathing, also known as four square breathing or box breathing, is a breathing exercise that will bring your body to a state of calm and stillness whenever you feel anxious, upset, frustrated, angry, nervous, etc. Any emotion that produces an unwanted physiological response can be better managed by engaging in the square breathing technique. Follow the following steps to experience the benefits of square breathing:

1. Slowly and silently count to four while taking a slow deep breath in through your nose.
2. Hold that inhalation for four slow counts.
3. Slowly and silently let the breath out to the count of four through your mouth.

4. Hold that exhalation for the count of four before starting over with step one and inhaling through your nose. Repeat 2-3 times.

This is a simple, yet very powerful and effective technique. You'll feel more relaxed in a matter of minutes. I've had clients share with me that they would engage in the square breathing technique whenever they found themselves in confrontations with others or challenging situations. They would always report on how amazed they were when they would notice the tension that typically accompanied these situations lessen tremendously.

Throughout your day make it a practice to occasionally stop what you are doing and savor your breathing. Consciously inhale slowly and deeply. As you exhale allow all the tension of the day to expel from your body. With each breath imagine yourself connecting with the Earth. Relish the feel-good sensations that are sure to resonate within you. Your body will appreciate the deliberate intention you make to connect with stillness.

MEDITATION

The benefits of meditation are invaluable. From a physiological standpoint, meditation balances many of the physiological processes that are impacted by our stressful lifestyles. It lowers blood pressure, pulse rates, and regulates breathing. From a mental perspective, meditation stills the mind. It reduces anxiety and alleviates feelings of depression. From a spiritual platform meditation activates and strengthens your intuition. It assists us in overcoming our perceived limitations and misconceptions we have of ourselves. Throughout history, philosophers, inventors and others utilized the power of meditation. Every problem has a solution and solutions are often times realized through the act of meditation. Many of these individuals touted meditation for its ability to open the channels of intuition leading the meditator to solutions, great discoveries, and indescribable experiences.

"The quieter you become, the more you can hear."
~ Baba Ram Dass

GOING UP BY GOING DOWN

Infinite wisdom including all of the information residing in your subconscious is accessible when you meditate. Meditation not only makes you more consciously aware, it allows you to tap into a higher consciousness. Many people call this God-consciousness. Paradoxically, we tap into this higher consciousness by lowering our physiological state. When your heart, breathing and respiratory rate goes down in meditation, your vibrational energy is raised very quickly. Thus, you go up by going down. When your vibrational energy is raised, you are connected to the information that is going to assist you in your transformation and success.

The power is in consistent meditation. You don't need more than 15-30 minutes a day, but it has to be consistent. Consistency forms the foundation that your meditative power will stand upon. Consistency in meditation establishes the intent to operate on a higher vibrational energy throughout the day. This pre-paves the day and directs your cells and your world in general to take it easy. It is impossible for joy, fulfillment or transformation to occur when you are not in alignment. When not in alignment, life becomes such a struggle. Consistent meditation guides you in the right path, the path of least resistance. Consistent meditation establishes a life of joy and fulfillment, the ultimate purpose of life. When you live life in a state of well-being, you become inspired and able to connect with that which is important for your alignment. That which will assist you and your transformation will flow right to you.

It is best to engage in meditation first thing in the morning, before life grabs you. Upon awakening, you are already in that relaxed state. When you get trapped in the busyness of the day, you will tell yourself, "I'm going to meditate, but I've got to get the kids to school. I'm going to meditate, but I've got to go to the grocery store. I'm going to meditate, but I must first make that appointment." Eventually it becomes, "I'm going to meditate before I go to sleep," and before you know it you're asleep and there goes your opportunity to meditate. You will abandon your intention to meditate each and every time if you don't make it a priority. Even in the most mundane day, there's a lot that we have to tend to. Commit to meditate first thing in the morning before the demands of life grab hold of you. The information that wants to channel through your subconscious is better able to do so when you consistently meditate. Information flows through to you so much easier, with far less effort.

DON'T GIVE UP

Meditation has been present for thousands of years yet continues to be a misunderstood concept, especially in western society. Upon learning all the wonderful benefits that exist in the practice, many will attempt to incorporate it into their lives. There is this desire to jump right in to immediately begin to tap into its benefit. It is typically at this point that one realizes that the act of meditating doesn't come as easily as one would want. It is soon discovered that quieting your busy mind is no small feat. Thoughts, memories, daydreams, and distractions will infiltrate the mind frustrating the novice meditator. Further attempts to master the practice may be met with even more persistent thoughts, memories, daydreams and distractions. Meditation then begins to be regarded as way too difficult a task. You feel like a failure at it and eventually abandon all efforts to meditate.

Meditation is called a practice because that is precisely what it requires to achieve a meditative state – practice. Your realization of your busy, incessant mind in your first attempts should not be regarded as a failure. To the contrary, it should be considered progress because now you realize that your struggle with stillness is not only external, but internal as well. The sooner you realize that this wandering quality of your mind is part of your mind's current nature the better. Once you realize this you are now better able to conquer it with further practice. You can release the feeling of defeat and focus on mastering the technique of stilling the mind. It's similar to a person who gets on a scale and realizes they have fifty pounds to lose. There is a sincere desire to lose the weight, so they begin exercising. The next day they get on the scale and realize there are still fifty pounds to lose. Discouraged because of the lack of instant results, many people will abandon their weight loss goals just as they abandon their meditation goals. Just as exercise is the best practice at shedding unnecessary weight, meditation is the best practice to still the mind. Your realization of how busy your mind is equivalent to you stepping on the scale. The mind chatter, thoughts, memories, judgment, noise, etc. are the fifty pounds of excess mental weight you are attempting to shed. It won't happen in a day's, week's or sometimes even month's time, but with consistent effort you will achieve it. Like exercise, meditation will require consistent efforts and you will progressively achieve the desired results.

Try not to get frustrated and give up when your mind wanders, it's going to happen, just as cravings will occur when you set out to lose weight. As you do with your cravings, you should aspire not to indulge in the mind chatter. Acknowledge that the mind chatter is there and return to the meditative state. The more you don't give in to your intrusive thoughts, the less powerful they become until eventually the mind chatter will disappear. Even when you slip up as you will and give in to your mind chatter don't dwell in it, simply acknowledge the thoughts are there and return to the meditative state. Distract and deter your thoughts by focusing back on your breathing. Be fully aware that your mind chatter, fearful that you are attempting to extinguish the control it has over you, will try even harder to distract you. Just as you would resist to giving in to temptation in your weight loss efforts, don't give in to the thoughts while meditating. Continue to shift the focus from your thoughts to your breathing and to the wonderful sensations your body is beginning to experience such as quietness, stillness, peace and connectedness. Don't expect too much in the beginning. Keep in mind, the more you practice, the better you become.

Your meditation location should be clean, quiet, and away from distractions. You may choose to add some object of inspiration or relaxation such as a candle, stone, etc. It is best to sit upright with straight posture, however, you may choose to lay. Whatever is most comfortable and most relaxing to you. You don't, however, want to be so relaxed that you fall asleep. There are plenty of guided meditation audio CDs available on the market that you can choose to start out with. Or you can also simply engage in and focus on deep, slow rhythmic breathing. Others may choose a particular chant or mantra as they meditate. The possibilities are many. Play around with it. Discover what resonates best with you and allow yourself to experience the transformative effects of stillness that can be achieved through meditation.

CHAPTER SEVEN

STEP 7: CONNECTEDNESS

"What is connectedness? It is a sense of being a part of something larger than oneself. It is a sense of belonging, or a sense of accompaniment. It is that feeling in your bones that you are not alone. It is a sense that, no matter how scary things may become, there is a hand for you in the dark. While ambition drives us to achieve, connectedness is my word for the force that urges us to ally, to affiliate, to enter into mutual relationships, to take strength and to grow through cooperative behavior."
~ Edward M. Hallowell

You can't be part of this world without some form of connectedness. The question is, what are you choosing to connect to? Are you connecting to people, thoughts and items? Are you connecting to your past, present or future? Are you connecting to beliefs, thought patterns, habits, people that are contrary to your transformation? Take a moment and evaluate connectedness in your life. Who are the people you connect to? What does your daily activities consist of? What is the quality of your daily conversations? Are they conversations whose overall content is one of gossip, fear or limitations? Your answer to these questions will provide you with the evidence of what your connectedness looks like. The fact is, what you connect to in your daily lives, through thoughts, words, and interactions will ALWAYS become your reality. You cannot experience anything that you aren't connected to.

At young ages most of us were taught the tangible things that we needed to connect to that would allow us to grab hold of the American Dream. We were all but guaranteed happiness and fulfillment if we connected to education, hard work, a spouse, and a family. Many of us abided and engaged in the tangible acts of working hard, becoming educated, getting married and acquiring the house on Main Street, but something went terribly wrong. We soon discovered that this American Dream that was promised to us, and imprinted on our psyche did not produce the happiness we expected. The American Dream, for many, has become a nightmare.

We were raised to believe only things we can observe, measure and see as real. That which we couldn't see, measure or experience through our senses was dismissed as irrelevant or even non-existent. Our heavy reliance on the tangible, influenced many religious practices with the insistence on attaching a tangible image of who would be worshiped. Our connection to the tangible has caused us to be far too one-sided in our existence. This has undoubtedly contributed to the general sense of discontent and disconnect that exists. What was failed to be taught to us were the intangibles that we could connect to that would ensure us as much or even more success and joy than those tangible things.

The unconscious living many of us have engaged in has resulted in most of us living a life where we unfortunately became connected to our thoughts and to tangible possessions. This tendency has led to the state of despair many people are experiencing. As we learned in Step 2, our connection to pathological thought pushed our conscious awareness out. All this constant thought has resulted in an inability to relax and as a result we have astronomical numbers of stress-related illnesses. Our connection to possessions has led to individuals being devastated and struggling with a loss of identity when their tangible possessions are taken from them. As it stands today, many are in a state of massive confusion as a result of the economic decline. The very things they connected to have been snatched away. For millions, the recession resulted in lost jobs, foreclosed homes, repossessed cars and wiped-out savings. Many regarded the loss of these material possessions as the end to life as they knew it. In some aspect, this regard was right. The recession for many was the beginning of the end of unconscious living. On a spiritual level, the recession as devastating as it seemed, had hidden blessings. Many of my clients, as a result of losing their home, relocated to parts of town or different parts of the country that they had for years desired to relocate to, but due to their connection to their homes never made the move. Many others who found themselves unemployed decided to pursue a career or education they had always desired to pursue, but because of seniority and the risk of walking away from their jobs, they opted to pursue their pension as opposed to their passion. I even had a client who finally lost the fifty pounds that he had wanted to lose for years after having his car repossessed and having to walk to many of the locations he used to so easily drive to.

In many ways, the beginning decade of the 21st century actually represents an ending. Recently, on a beautiful Sunday morning, I visited a church I had never been to. As I settled in my seat, I felt a sense of encouragement and hope as the choir sang. The combination of chords, beats, and rhythms was comforting. The music had me empowered. After the choir's last musical selection, the very distinguished, proud-looking minister approached the pulpit. I straightened my posture, hungrily anticipating his message. I thought to myself, if the music had me feeling this empowered then surely the minister's sermon would have me feeling as though I could take on the world.

As the minister adjusted his microphone, I scanned the room noticing all the other parishioners, who, like me, seemed to be on the edge of their seats. All eyes were fixated, eagerly awaiting his message. As if he was aware of our hungry anticipation, he took his time and very calmly and methodically organized his notes on the podium, cleared his throat and in the deepest, most bass-filled voice, proclaimed in a very dramatic, apocalyptic fashion, "Ladies and gentlemen, we are in our last days." He went on to speak for the next thirty minutes on how the wrath of God was upon us. The energy in the room immediately shifted from one of empowered optimism to one of hopeless dread. Faces, that just minutes earlier were filled with smiles and satisfaction instantly became anxious, despondent and defeated. It was as though someone had attached a giant vacuum to the doors of the church and sucked all the life out.

In the minister's defense, I honestly don't believe it was his intent to horrify us. In fact, this was not the first time I had witnessed religious leaders proclaiming the end of humanity in this spectacular approach. For many, this is their best interpretation of the uncertainty, unsettled and unconscious world we live in. Real life occurrences of increased crime, financial despair, recessions, failing education, increased substance abuse, growing prisons serve as examples as a sure-tell sign that the end of civility is near.

My interpretation however differs from the fatalistic interpretation offered by many including this minister. I do not believe we are in a fast lane, one-way course to damnation. We are not in our last days. I do believe, however, that we are nearing an end of an era. We are collectively nearing an end stage of a collective, unconscious, disconnected existence whose characteristics could easily be confused as our last days.

Allow me to draw upon a pregnancy analogy to further explain myself. Having four children of my own, I am quite familiar with the process of pregnancy and childbirth. When a woman becomes pregnant, there are 40 weeks of gestation in which the fetus develops, acquiring all that is necessary to be viable outside of its mother's womb. The last century can be equated to a time of gestation, coming off the heels of slavery, the industrial revolution, civil rights movement, space travel and a technological revolution whose innovations leaves us awe-struck. We have achieved and mastered so much that makes our lives viable yet there continues to be so much uncertainty, despair and disconnect.

Returning to the pregnancy analogy, there comes a time in a fetus's gestation when the womb is no longer viable, when remaining one day longer could prove fatal to both mother and child. We are in a time when our gestation is complete and the birth of a new consciousness is not only imminent, but absolutely necessary. We have in essence gestated. We have acquired massive amounts of information that has catapulted our evolution, and now is the time for a re-birth. We must connect once again to our natural state of being, that of conscious awareness.

Much like the labor pains that begin when the fetus's time in the womb is complete, we are collectively feeling an instinctive need to push through. The birth of a new mindset, a new consciousness is now. Gestation is complete. The labor pains have begun (strife in the world, civil and financial unrest, personal discontent). Contractions are becoming closer and closer with no break in between (one perceived personal and world tragedy after another) and many have become crippled with discomfort (choosing to suppress their emotional discontent with illegal and legal substances). The time is now for you to bear down and push. Many now stand at a fork in the road. A decision must be made to either take that final push or remain in a state that will be sure to have far reaching devastating consequences on an individual and global level.

The time has come for a collective shift in consciousness. A shift from disconnected unconsciousness to one of connected conscious awareness. Collectively, we cannot afford to continue to live life by the same rules. That would be like trying to put a size nine foot in a size seven shoe. It just won't fit. The failing educational system, growing prisons, obesity crisis, breakdown of the family, and economic despair can all be attributed to us applying outdated approaches to 21st century living. It is crucial that we disconnect from the reality that has had our attention for quite some time and connect to that truth that lies in conscious awareness.

The time has come to self-correct, to incorporate the practices that will manifest success in your life. Over the past few years there has been an avalanche of books that have addressed the concepts of conscious awareness, the law of attraction, power of thoughts, etc. Many of these books address the same phenomenon. I recall a professor in my first year of undergrad discussing the concept of *zeitgeist*. I had never heard that word before, but it fascinated me. He explained how zeitgeist means a trend of thought. It's sort of a collective gut feeling that may exist in a period of time. The professor shared how common it was for a scientist in one corner of the world to be uncovering some new invention while in a completely opposite corner of the world another scientist could be uncovering the same fascinating invention at the same time. These scientists could be totally oblivious to each other. There are accounts of scientists in other areas of the world stumbling upon electricity at roughly the same time Edison did. Some may explain this as coincidence, however according to zeitgeist when the time comes for some new invention or mindset to be introduced to our world that is crucial to our evolution, our connected consciousness will see to it that it is developed. You will find people all over the world coming up with similar concepts resulting in paradigm shifts. The 21st century has introduced us to a level of connectedness we've never experienced. As we are compelled to reconnect with our expanding consciousness we are seeing more and more extraordinary examples of connectedness. Consider the Internet and social media as prime examples. The world has become exponentially more accessible as our connectedness and conscious awareness is reclaimed.

In the last decade, the zeitgeist of connectedness via conscious awareness and the law of attraction has infiltrated books, lectures, documentaries and coffee house conversations. We must pay attention to this zeitgeist for it suggests that incorporating these concepts in our lives is crucial to our growth, evolution and ultimate success.

As discussed in Chapter Two, living consciously makes you aware of the infinite connections that exist in your life. When you are consciously aware, you are better able to disconnect from that which is contrary to your success and connect to the highest potential that resides within you. Conscious awareness is God awareness. It's like having a direct line to the storehouse of knowledge that has always resided within you but somehow became buried in a lifetime of unconscious living.

THE LAW OF ATTRACTION

A Google search of the law of attraction yields nearly 17 million results. It is not surprising that so many have expressed sincere interest in exploring and utilizing this natural law. Unlike the law of gravity, the law of attraction was never taught in our science classes. It wasn't taught in the home. Nevertheless, this law is being utilized by every single human being on the face of this earth either constructively or destructively. Most are unknowingly using it and deriving results that maintain undesirable states. The law simply implies that which we connect to comes back to us. It is a sort of boomerang effect. It asserts that to some degree, we play a role in whatever happens to us. We are typically willing to accept some responsibility for the good things that happens to us. None of us, however, want to accept any responsibility for the bad things that happen. The law of attraction doesn't distinguish between good and bad, it simply returns what you put out.

This law is the very reason it is more important than ever to align yourself with people, thoughts, attitudes and emotions that represent what you want more of. Surrounding yourself with people who are critical and negative will only bring you more criticism and negativity in all areas of your life. Connecting with thoughts of lack and limitation can only yield more lack and limitation. Discriminating, condemning attitudes will bring about those violations in your life. Anger, rage, sadness and fear will continually introduce you to situations in which those emotions are present. You will always be in alignment with the condition you radiate in the world. The law of attraction is an energy that goes out and seeks the same energy to return it to you. As we learned with affirmations, you must take care that whatever you are radiating out is what you desire to get back in return.

This is a hard pill to swallow for many, because there is a sort of comfort that has been derived from not owning responsibility for the multitude of misfortune that happens in our lives. It is so much easier to present yourself as a victim who like a leaf in the wind has no control over the direction it's blown. When you understand the law of attraction you realize that you have always been the wind.

One of the benefits of the law of attraction is that you can never live in harmony with a thought, person, attitude or emotion that you are not in alignment with. People who are generally optimistic, joyful and happy cannot stay in a place of despair for long. We see it as the person pulling themselves up by the boot straps, however the law of attraction explains that it's simply the person getting back into their predominant disposition and attraction that which they are.

I regularly witness the law of attraction in effect with my clients, particularly when it comes to relationships. They will express chronic dissatisfaction with their partner, constant bickering and an inability to see eye-to-eye. Truth is, it is impossible for you to live in harmony with someone you are not in alignment with. Say for instance, you are operating on a higher, more positive vibrational energy than your partner. One of two things will happen in this situation. You will either have to lower your vibrational energy down to connect with the more negative, pessimistic person or that person will have to raise their vibrational energy up to connect to your more positive, optimistic disposition. It is much harder for a person to raise their vibration up to a level they've never been. It is next to impossible for a person to become positive and optimistic and stay there if they have not done the self work necessary to raise vibrationally. The all too often unfortunate result is the higher vibrational, more optimistic person lowering their vibration, thus becoming more negative and pessimistic so they can eliminate the disharmony in their relationship. The misery thus finds its company.

Kendra was a client of mine who had always considered herself positive and happy. Bill, her husband of ten years, had progressively become more cynical over the course of their marriage. They were constantly in a vibrational tug of war with Kendra wanting Bill to connect to her vibrational disposition of happiness and positivity and Bill wanting Kendra to take off her rose colored glasses and see the world as he did—uncertain and depressing. Throughout the ten years of marriage each would give in vibrationally with Kendra periodically connecting with Bill's vibrational energy and vice versa. However, the vibrational equilibrium they would occasionally experience was always short lived. Kendra stated it never felt good when she would agree with her husband's worldview to achieve harmony in her marriage. Operating outside of your true vibrational set point can never bring harmony because doing so compromises your connection. Never lower your vibrational energy to meet someone at their point of growth. This leads to regression and will prevent growth for you as well as the other person involved. When you do this, you can only attract what the lower level person is capable of attracting. Individuals who have found themselves in this situation often complain how they never seem to get ahead. These same individuals will express a feeling of relief when they free themselves from the lower vibrational pull. It is amazing how life can and will transform for individuals who are courageous enough to walk away from the perpetual tug-of-war and reclaim their positive, optimistic vibrational set point. Your success or lack thereof in life is indeed connected to the people you surround yourself with.

HOW WILL I KNOW IF I'M BECOMING MORE CONNECTED?

As you become more connected to that which is in alignment with your destiny, you will become more and more plugged in to the natural rhythm of the universe. Things will feel more aligned. Life will require less effort. The rat race, the tug-of-war will not be part of your reality. You will become like a magnet, attracting the things to you that will ensure your destiny and purpose are fulfilled. It will seem as though you've been given access to a smorgasbord of opportunities that come to you with far less effort than you've ever imagined. As a result, it will be increasingly difficult to be in the presence of others who continue to choose an unconscious, disconnected existence. Being in their presence will feel toxic. The law of attraction will not allow you to coexist with individuals for any significant amounts of time. These people will be the kryptonite to your newfound Superman.

In the following table indicate the people you regularly interact with. List their names in the first column. In the second column, indicate if that person's vibrational energy matches or differs from yours. If the energy differs, in the third column indicate if you would need to lower or raise your vibrational energy to match that person.

People You Regularly Interact with	Vibrational Quality matches or differs (circle one)	Will you need to raise or lower your vibration to match
1	matches differs	raise lower
2	matches differs	raise lower
3	matches differs	raise lower
4	matches differs	raise lower
5	matches differs	raise lower
6	matches differs	raise lower
7	matches differs	raise lower

8	matches differs	raise lower
9	matches differs	raise lower
10	matches differs	raise lower

Consider the results of this table. Is there constant struggle and strife with those individuals whose vibrational energy is not a match for you? For the relationships that require you to lower your vibrational energy to achieve harmony, ask yourself if you are willing to do so. If so, what do you believe the personal ramifications of lowering your vibrational energy would be? For the relationships that will require you to raise your vibrational energy to achieve harmony, start doing the work of the seven steps to begin connecting to your transformation.

HOW TO ACHIEVE CONNECTEDNESS
1. Identify what it is in life that you want to connect to.
Be clear and specific. Use the knowledge you've gained about yourself in the six previous steps as a guide. Refer to your vision board and affirmations to further clarify your desired connectedness.

2. Get into alignment with it.

Once you have identified your desires, get into alignment with them. You must speak it, breathe it and align yourself with the people, thoughts, emotions and environment that are consistent with those desires.

3. Accept the ease.

Once you are in alignment, your connectedness will occur effortlessly. Only then will you experience the supernatural ease and flow that will become the theme song of your life. Just as you don't have to tell the law of gravity to operate, the law of attraction won't need your help. It will operate with ease as it has always operated in your life. The only difference now is your awareness.

EPILOGUE

PREPARE FOR TAKE-OFF

The miracle of flight never ceases to amaze me. Hundreds of people defying gravity in a metal tube transporting themselves from one point to another still boggles my mind. In my recent travels I reflected upon the concept of air travel and it seemed such a perfect analogy to what happens when we decide to embark upon transformation in our lives. Consider what is required for a plane to transport our physical bodies from one location to a typically more desired destination. We board the plane, take our seat and buckle in. It is necessary for us to fasten our seat belts because there is sure to be some turbulence as we soar to higher altitudes. Just as there will be some turbulence as you begin your journey towards transformation, your take off cannot be passive. Planes that passively move along the runway will never take flight. A plane must build up momentum before it can defy the law of gravity and leave the ground. Just as you must commit, here and now to gather the momentum necessary for your transformation to occur, the time is now for you to defy and dispel the thoughts, practices and beliefs that have kept you grounded. As you began reading this book, you were on the tarmac, awaiting direction from the control tower. The seven steps are the control tower telling you it is all clear to proceed. Allow the direction they provide to motivate and inspire you to create the momentum to take off to altitudes that will literally take your breath away.

The steps presented in this book are tools that when utilized properly will connect you to your destiny. Utilized individually they are powerful, however, utilized together they are transformative. We all want something to believe in that can give life more meaning, that can lessen the suffering Confucius proclaimed life to be. *Bloom* is your revelation to an extraordinary life. Now that you have this revelation, you can't go backwards. You can't pretend you don't know something that you know. Revelations give you freedom from the illusion. What I have discovered in my research, in my practice, and in my firsthand experience is that contentment, joy, bliss, and true serenity is possible. This place of conscious, extraordinary living is, and will forever be, accessible to us all.

ABOUT THE AUTHOR

Dr. Rose Moten is a clinical psychologist and life coach in private practice. She is passionately committed to helping others achieve extraordinary success in life. Through both verbal and written dialogue, she shares proven strategies for personal growth and transformation. Dr. Rose has served as keynote speaker for numerous organizations and has been featured on national television and radio programs as well as in newsprint articles.

Contact The Author:

Email: DrRoseMoten@DrRoseMoten.com

Website: www.DrRoseMoten.com

Facebook Page: In Full Bloom with Dr. Rose

Twitter: @DrRoseMoten

25083515R00119

Made in the USA
Middletown, DE
16 October 2015